At Issue

Does the World Hate the U.S.?

Other Books in the At Issue Series:

At Issue

Does the World Hate the U.S.?

Roman Espejo, Book Editor

GREENHAVEN PRESS
A part of Gale, Cengage Learning

GALE
CENGAGE Learning™

Detroit • New York • San Francisco • New Haven, Conn • Waterville, Maine • London

Christine Nasso, *Publisher*
Elizabeth Des Chenes, *Managing Editor*

© 2009 Greenhaven Press, a part of Gale, Cengage Learning.

Gale and Greenhaven Press are registered trademarks used herein under license.

For more information, contact:
Greenhaven Press
27500 Drake Rd.
Farmington Hills, MI 48331-3535
Or you can visit our Internet site at gale.cengage.com

For product information and technology assistance, contact us at

Gale Customer Support, 1-800-877-4253
For permission to use material from this text or product, submit all requests online at
www.cengage.com/permissions

Further permissions questions can be emailed to permissionrequest@cengage.com

Articles in Greenhaven Press anthologies are often edited for length to meet page require-ments. In addition, original titles of these works are changed to clearly present the main thesis and to explicitly indicate the author's opinion. Every effort is made to ensure that Greenhaven Press accurately reflects the original intent of the authors. Every effort has been made to trace the owners of copyrighted material.

Cover photograph reproduced by permission of © Images.com/Corbis.

LIBRARY OF CONGRESS CATALOGING-IN-PUBLICATION DATA

Does the world hate the U.S.? / Roman Espejo, book editor.
    p. cm. -- (At issue)
Includes bibliographical references and index.
ISBN 978-0-7377-4096-7 (hardcover)
ISBN 978-0-7377-4097-4 (pbk.)
1. Anti-Americanism. 2. United States--Foreign public opinion. 3. United States--Foreign relations--2001- 4. United States--Relations--Foreign countries. 5. Civiliza-tion, Modern--American influences. I. I. Espejo, Roman, 1977-
    E895.D64 2008
    973.93--dc22

                                                                    2008022301

Printed in the United States of America
2 3 4 5 6 7 12 11 10 09

Contents

Introduction

Having reached its fifth year in March 2008, the U.S.-led Iraq war has emerged as a major topic of editorials, papers, and research on anti-Americanism today. Perhaps most famously, a 2006 report by the Pew Research Center contends that favorable opinions of the United States have not nearly reached the heights they did in 1999 and 2000, asserting that the Iraq war is inextricably linked to the continuing decline of the United States' reputation around the world:

America's global image has again slipped and support for the war on terrorism has declined even among close U.S. allies like Japan. The war in Iraq is a continuing drag on opinions of the United States, not only in predominantly Muslim countries but in Europe and Asia as well. And despite growing concern over Iran's nuclear ambitions, the U.S. presence in Iraq is cited at least as often as Iran—and in many countries much more often—as a danger to world peace.

Furthermore, in a special series published by the *Chronicle of Higher Education* in November 2002, numerous scholars predicted that the then-anticipated war on Iraq would deepen global anti-American sentiment by 2007. According to John L. Esposito, professor of religion and international affairs at Georgetown University,

To move to a military strike before exhausting nonmilitary avenues, and without significant multilateral support from our European and Arab/Muslim allies, as well as from the United Nations, will have inflamed anti-Americanism, which will have grown exponentially in the region and the non-Muslim world and will have reinforced the growing perception that the United States has become an imperial power that is attempting to redraw the map of the Middle East and, perhaps, the Muslim world.

In addition, in one of the two scenarios he presented, Joseph S. Nye Jr., dean of Harvard University's Kennedy School of Government, darkly speculated that by October 2007, the United States would have suffered its third major terrorist attack, which would have "cost thousands of American lives, shaken investor confidence in the world economy, and further strained our bonds with Europe."

Not all of these scholars, however, agreed that the Iraq war would be a detriment to America's image. Barry Rubin, director of Global Research in International Affairs, claimed that "new issues and events would arise, making the Iraq war less important in determining regional attitudes toward the United States." "The current volume of anti-American propaganda," he continued, "could hardly be raised higher." Furthermore, countering "conventional-wisdom arguments" against the Iraq war, he resoundingly suggested that American political and military intervention in the country—ruled then by the late dictator Saddam Hussein—could actually improve perceptions of the United States:

> In reality, Middle Eastern anti-Americanism has much in common with the anti-Americanism that previously ruled the Communist world. Once people consider their dictators to be vulnerable, they may stop accepting the distraction of anti-Americanism and focus on their real problems and true tormentors. And once the dictatorships fall—as was seen in Russia—the anti-Americanism they fostered dissipates with remarkable speed.

In March 2008, the scholars reexamined the Iraq war and anti-Americanism predictions they had written for the *Chronicle of Higher Education*. Reflecting on his forecast, Esposito says,

> It is both satisfying and yet depressing that my predictions five years ago have in fact been realized. Anti-Americanism has grown exponentially in the Muslim world as it has in

many other parts of the world. Thus, the question "Why do they hate us?" remains important to ponder.

What is more compelling, however, is Rubin's reaction to the optimistic outlook he put forth in November 2002: "Regrettably, my worst fears about the cost in American prestige and credibility, as well as a return to the old, bad analysis of the [Middle East], have come true. . . . There were no easy answers in 2003; there are none now."

The scholars who participated in the *Chronicle of Higher Education* series may have come to a closer consensus that, five years on, the Iraq war has damaged some global opinions of the United States. Yet, not all share the same perspectives on whether the war has fueled anti-Americanism across the world. In *At Issue: Does the World Hate the U.S.?*, scholars, experts, and others offer their viewpoints on the Iraq war and other cited causes of anti-Americanism as well as its history and patterns. Moreover, they investigate possible strategies to ease anti-American sentiment abroad while protecting the interests of the United States and the well-being of its people.

1

What Is Anti-Americanism?

Nicole Speulda

Nicole Speulda is project director at the Pew Research Center for the People & the Press in Washington, D.C.

Anti-Americanism is a complex phenomenon that is dependent on several factors: U.S. foreign policies and engagement in global affairs, its use of military force against other countries, and the influence and reach of its popular culture. In recent years, the terrorist attacks of September 11, 2001, and the Iraq war have predominantly shaped the world's views of the United States, with extensive polls showing that the U.S.-led invasion of Iraq has eroded the support the United States gained from the terrorist attacks. Also, looming problems of globalization, which is often synonymous among many countries with Americanization, have further tarnished the world's views of the United States and its people. Anti-Americanism is a worsening threat that the country can no longer ignore.

Defining anti-Americanism is a complex task and means many things to different people. For some, being "against" America means disagreement with American policies, for others America is inextricably entwined with "globalization" and the spreading of specific cultural products; for others it is being against American leadership and for some it signifies opposition to American military power. In most cases it is more than one complaint. The purpose of this [viewpoint] is to document the phenomenon of anti-Americanism by examining the image of America, its people, policies and its perceived influence in the world.

Nicole Speulda, "Documenting the Phenomenon of Anti-Americanism," *The Princeton Project on National Security*, 2005.

[One thing] to keep in mind when analyzing "anti-Americanism" is that it inscribes a combination of complaints, not one particular problem a single nation or group of people has with America. And, let's keep in mind America has been down this road before, quite prophetically summed up in 1983:

> The most telling generalization that can be drawn from the poll results is that Americans are seen as a good and productive people with an erratic or even dangerous government. And while the policies of the Reagan administration—like those of some of its predecessors—heighten skepticism about American power and intentions, the world guilelessly embraces America's products and popular culture.[1]

Anti-Americanism can no longer be thought of as an isolated phenomenon; it's a global one.

But the kind of anti-American sentiments being voiced today are more troublesome than those in 1983. As public opinion surveys increase their scope and incorporate more countries, they also chart trends, ongoing measures of the same question that allows for in-depth analysis. Why are anti-American attitudes more troubling now? They are becoming increasingly entrenched in countries that have traditionally held negative views of the U.S. as well as among long-term American allies. Anti-Americanism can no longer be thought of as an isolated phenomenon; it's a global one.

U.S. Favorability Ratings

In a 2002 survey of 38,000 people in 44 countries the Pew Research Center found U.S. favorability ratings had slipped in most countries for which trends were available. This slide was considerable among America's traditional allies (Britain,

---

1. "What the World Thinks of America," *Newsweek*, July 11, 1983.

France, Germany and Italy) as well as the predominantly Muslim countries to which the U.S. looked for support in the war on terrorism—Turkey, Pakistan and Indonesia. In May 2003, just after the war in Iraq, the U.S. image plummeted, particularly in Muslim countries surveyed. Newspaper headlines screamed "Fear and Loathing," regarding how the world viewed America.

The phenomenon was not limited to a few countries. Surveys have shown publics in Latin America less favorable of the United States in recent times. In Brazil, attitudes toward the U.S. dropped 12 points in a year between 2002 and 2003.

U.S. favorability ratings (those saying they had a "very favorable" or "somewhat favorable" opinion of the United States) fell below 50% in France, Germany, Spain and even Russia. In Indonesia, Turkey and Pakistan ratings were 15% favorable or lower; Lebanon, Jordan and Morocco were equally abysmal with 27% in both Lebanon and Morocco holding a positive view and a mere 1% of Jordanians holding a favorable view.

In a survey in March 2004, a year after the war began, [there was] no improvement in favorability of America, and [it was] even worsening in Europe. The British favorability number went from seven-in-ten positive in May 2003 to 58% in March 2004. All other publics surveyed had lower numbers and no other country had a majority favorable rating of the U.S. . . .

Young people express more antipathy for America than their older cohorts in most of the West.

The U.S. image has slipped most in Turkey, where favorable ratings are currently 23%, half as high as they were in 1999, and in Canada where the 59% favorable rating continues to fall from 63% in 2003 and 72% in 2002.

Analyses of the 2002 data have shown remarkably few differences of opinion toward the United States nor any pattern of gender differences or generational gaps in U.S. favorability. However, the same is not the case today. Younger people express more antipathy for America than their older cohorts in most of the West. For example, in 2002 38% in France under age 30 had an unfavorable opinion of the U.S. and by 2005, 64% view[ed] America negatively. In Britain, America's closest ally in the war on terrorism, animosity among the young has doubled—from one-in-six in 2002 to one-in-three in 2005. A similar rise in the dislike of America is seen in Germany and it is even more pronounced in Spain; fully 62% of Spaniards under age 30 have a negative view of the U.S. while just 39% of their elders say so.

Much of this can be correlated with U.S. policies, particularly the war in Iraq. Independent polls commissioned by media organizations in France, Spain and Germany showed younger people [to be more opposed to] the war than older people and more of the very vocal protestors demonstrating across Europe in the run-up to the March [2003] invasion were of the younger generation. However, even if youthful opposition to the United States is just a passing fad, it is still troublesome in that it could pose a longer-term problem for American foreign policy in the future.

The Primary Focus

President [George W.] Bush has been the primary focus of much disdain among the young, but in this regard, they are not so different from their older cohorts. Those registering an "unfavorable" opinion of the U.S. were asked a follow-up asking why they held this view. Was it a general problem with America, or was it mostly because of President Bush? Low esteem for President Bush is the single variable most highly correlated with the unfavorable image of the United States not just among European publics, but throughout almost all of the publics polled. In 2003 majorities in Western Europe and Canada said it was Bush, however, 58% of Russians and 49%

of Poles said their negative view was a more general problem with America. In the 2005 Pew study, that question was posed again and in most countries surveyed, the problem with America increased and Bush being the cause of their unfavorable feelings toward America decreased. While Bush and his policies may have been an early focal point of people's negative attitudes, clearly America's image problem is much bigger than Bush.

American Views of the U.S.

Yet, Americans have no illusions about their image among global publics. Fully 69% of the American public said the U.S. was generally disliked by countries around the world, by far the lowest of any of the other 16 countries polled in 2005. Only in two other countries surveyed, Turkey and Russia, do a majority say their country is disliked and strong majorities in most all other countries believe themselves to be popular in the eyes of the rest of the world.

The unpopularity of Americans is not lost on the public, nor is it lost on the American and international media. The fact that China was given higher favorability ratings than the U.S. among European countries headlined major news outlets around the world. . . .

Yet favorability ratings of the U.S. in general cannot tell us about overall opinions regarding the American people and they don't tell us anything about which aspects of American policies the world dislikes. The next sections will parse those out.

Global Views of Americans

Historically, public opinion of the United States as a country has been more negative than attitudes regarding the American people. The 1983 Newsweek International survey reported approval of the American people much higher in all six countries surveyed (France, Germany, Britain, Brazil, Mexico and

Japan) than approval of U.S. policies or the "American way of life." While this is still the case, in several countries around the world, the gap has narrowed. In the 2005 Pew survey, Americans are seen less favorably in 9 of the 12 countries for which there is trend data. A similar German Marshall Fund survey in 2004 showed nearly identical results.

Just as favorability ratings for the U.S. are often conflated with United States policies, favorability of Americans may be inseparable from what they produce or who they elect. Attitudes have fallen regarding the American public and some of this may have to with the election of Bush. Global publics say they have a more favorable opinion of the U.S. for its efforts to aid the victims [of the Indian Ocean tsunami in] December [2004], at the same time they have a far less favorable attitude toward America for electing Bush to a second term.

For the first time it seems that Americans are being held to account for who they vote for by an international public. While people around the world see good in aid for other countries, they are not in favor of many Bush policies and are beginning to show signs of attributing American leadership to Americans.

Also, Pew surveys have found that in countries such as Indonesia, Russia, Turkey and Pakistan, where American people are increasingly viewed unfavorably, Americans are beginning to look more like [the] overall opinion of the United States. If Americans (and therefore American life) are no longer distinguishable from American policy, the U.S. government may have a larger problem on its hands.

Religion

How people around the world regard America, its people, and what it symbolizes to them is based on a multiplicity of factors. What's more, this combination of factors is viewed diametrically in different parts of the world. One such example is with regard to how the world sees the role of religion in

America. While more secular Europeans criticize America as being too religious a country, Muslim publics think America is not religious enough. This is one area in which Americans agree with their harshest critics; 58% of Americans say the U.S. is not religious enough and only 21% [say] their country is [too] religious. Moreover, fully 80% of evangelical Christians say America is not religious enough, more than the Turks (60%), Lebanese (61%), Pakistanis (63%) and Indonesians (69%). Only in Jordan do beliefs about America's lack of religion match evangelical Christians, with 95% saying Americans are not religious enough.

However, agreeing with U.S. public opinion with regard to American religiosity is still a criticism, just as is having the traits of being immoral and violent. And, particularly in predominantly Muslim countries where opinions like these translate directly into U.S. policies regarding Iraq and to being targets of the U.S. war on terrorism, not being religious enough is a sign of wanting to spread the secular nature of American capitalism rather than any virtuous-based valued democracy to a particular country.

Oh, Canada. . .

Canadian esteem for America and its people has fallen precipitously in the last few years as shown in the opinions of America's neighbor to the north. Canadians are increasingly negative about all things American. Canadian opinion of the American people has seen a 12 percent decrease since 2002 and, while [in 1999] more than seven-in-ten Canadians held a favorable view of the United States, that has steadily diminished to just over half (59%) in 2005. What's more, majorities in Canada see Americans as greedy, violent and rude and, as discussed later, they are not happy with U.S. policies. Such negative opinions across the board demonstrate that American foreign policy is having an effect on overall attitudes toward the United States and is bleeding into the way Canadians see the American people.

The American Character

While Canadians are among Americans' biggest critics, elsewhere around the world, opinion of the U.S. character is mixed. In Pew's 2005 survey, publics in 16 countries *and* the U.S. were given a rotating list of seven character traits (hardworking, inventive and honest, greedy, violent, rude and immoral). A majority in every country (except China) associates "hardworking" with Americans and a majority in all countries believes Americans are "inventive." There is less of a consensus whether Americans are honest; only in the U.S., India, Britain, France and Germany do more than half the publics describe Americans that way.

However, even Americans are willing to say their fellow Americans are greedy, with 70% saying so and nearly half (49%) say Americans are violent. In general, people in predominantly Muslim countries surveyed hold more negative views of Americans than traditional allies, but most countries say violent is an American trait. Only in the Muslim countries (Jordan, Lebanon, Pakistan, Turkey and Indonesia) do at least half of respondents say Americans are immoral.

Europeans are less likely to associate negative traits with Americans than other countries surveyed. Only about a third of the French think Americans are greedy and slightly more believe Americans to be immoral. And, far fewer British say Americans are immoral or rude than others surveyed. Yet, half or more Europeans see Americans as violent people.

Again, this ambivalence regarding how global publics view Americans is not necessarily a new phenomenon. Similar results were catalogued in the 1983 Newsweek poll which found majorities in Britain, Germany, France and Mexico saying Americans were "self-indulgent," and the same majorities in those countries associated Americans with being "energetic."

These numbers show that opinions of Americans and the image of what being American may entail, have remained largely unchanged. There has never been a consensus among

European publics as to what comprises the American character. That Americans can be inventive and honest does not mean that they can't also be greedy and violent. Global publics are able to distinguish between the characteristics they find unbecoming of America and Americans. . . .

War on Terrorism

The war on terrorism has proven more problematic than beneficial for the United States. In 2002, when the United States was still reeling from the 9/11 terror attacks, Europeans in the East and West were highly supportive of the war on terrorism, as were publics in Africa, and majorities in 7 of 8 Latin American countries. In Nigeria, three quarters of the public favored the U.S.-led efforts to fight terrorism, 65% of Indians were in favor and over 90% of Uzbeks supported the U.S. policy. However, most Muslim publics surveyed were not so keen on the war on terrorism with 79% in Egypt, 85% in Jordan and majorities in Lebanon and Turkey opposed to the war on terrorism.

By 2003 support began to wane across Europe, and opposition increased among Muslim publics. Even public opinion polls in the U.S. have shown a steady decline in support for the war on terrorism and Americans are now split as to whether or not the war in Iraq has helped or hurt the war on terrorism. In 2005, European support for U.S. efforts to fight terrorism continued to fall; in Spain support fell 37 points despite Spain's own experience with terror bombings. More Canadians now oppose the war than support it. Even in India, where the U.S. image has remained quite positive in the past three years, support for the war on terrorism has fallen 13 percentage points.

Much of the drop in support comes as a result of the war in Iraq. But it also stems from the fact that larger percentages in Europe believe the U.S. is overreacting to the threat terrorism presents. And, for some countries, particularly among

Muslim populations, there is a real fear that they could be the next target of the war on terrorism.

The Iraq War

The spring of 2003 was a contentious one; the United States invaded Iraq without U.N. approval and with much international protest particularly in Europe—among both supporters of the "war on terrorism" and those opposed to it. Among countries who decided to abstain from joining the U.S. coalition, public opinions say that decision was a good one. In Canada, for example, 65% approved of their government's decision not to use force, and two years later, fully eight-in-ten say it was the right decision. While British and American publics stood by their countries' decision to use force in Iraq, the number in both countries has fallen considerably. In Pew's 2005 survey just 39% of Britons believe sending troops to Iraq was the right one and just over half of Americans say so.

The war in Iraq has hurt U.S. credibility and global publics now say America is less trustworthy, and that American and British leaders lied when they claimed Iraq had WMD [weapons of mass destruction]. Most countries in Europe and among predominantly Muslim countries surveyed question America's motives for using force in Iraq, believing the invasion was not to rid Iraq of weapons of mass destruction but to control Middle East oil supplies and to dominate the world.

The U.S. is also resented for being the world's only superpower.

Differing Views on Security Issues

The past two and a half years of Pew Global Attitudes surveys have shown profound differences in not only how Americans and the rest of the world view threats but how to deal with those threats. Majorities in the Western European countries surveyed believe their own government should obtain U.N. approval before dealing with an international threat. That idea is much more problematic for Americans, with a 48% plurality saying that U.N. approval would make it too difficult to deal with international threats.

The 2004 German Marshall Fund survey found America holding very different opinions with nearly all European publics regarding the use of force. The U.S. public is far more willing to use force and go-it-alone, unlike Europeans who do not share that view. Nearly half of Americans *strongly agree* that war is sometimes necessary to obtain justice. Only about one-in-ten in Germany, France and Italy say the same and majorities in those countries disagree that war is necessary to obtain justice. A majority of Americans also believe that the best way to ensure peace is through military strength, and again, Europeans disagree. These differing attitudes regarding the use of force show why the war in Iraq and the way in which the U.S. wields its power are disturbing to Europeans.

The U.S. is also resented for being the world's only superpower. Acting unilaterally and not taking others' interests into account causes publics around the globe to see the U.S. as abusing its superpower status. A European Union poll of all member publics indicated that 53% sees the United States as a threat to world peace, the same number as who saw North Korea and Iran as a threat. . . .

Majorities in all 16 countries surveyed in 2005 say it would be better if another power rivaled U.S. military power, to add as a check against the U.S. Americans do not agree, a 63% majority preferring a uni-polar world.

America's Global Reach and Lifestyle in a Globalizing World

Historically, America's image was synonymous with individual opportunity, hope and a place other ethnicities could come to seek their fortune. Yet the exceptional American dream described by [French historian] Alexis de Tocqueville in his *Democracy in America*, is no longer the European ideal and certainly not the global ideal. In a 2005 Pew survey, respondents were asked to name one country they would recommend a young person go to lead a better life, and only one country, India, named the U.S. as their top choice.

Overload of American culture may be one explanation for the [decline] of the country's popularity in a variety of aspects. Globalization, increased flow of ideas, trade and people across borders is often associated with "Americanization," countries saturated with American popular culture and business models. People all over the world say they have seen the impact of globalization in their countries yet they say they think it's a bad thing that U.S. ideas and customs are spreading there. Similarly, on average, only a third of Canadians, Britons, French, Italians and Germans say they like American ways of doing business. Also, publics throughout Latin America and Europe are wary of American ideas about democracy. In many countries, such as Argentina, Brazil and France, majorities dislike American democratic ideas. The predominantly Muslim publics of Turkey, Pakistan and Jordan also dislike American democracy.

When America feels threatened, people around the world worry about their own safety and the possible repercussions of U.S. policies.

However, this is not the case everywhere. In ten countries of Africa, majorities (in some cases very strong majorities) express positive views of American ideas about democracy. And, while many Muslim countries dislike American ideas about democracy, they do believe that "western-style" could work in their countries. Democratic ideals do not belong only to the United States, but it is shared among countries all over the world. It is the imposition of "democracy" that they fear.

The Larger Struggle to Defend

The world in which we live is an ever-changing one and it is too early to predict how the U.S. will be viewed in the future. Much hinges on a positive outcome in Iraq and successful diplomatic efforts by the U.S., its traditional allies and countries worldwide to repair relationships and mutual trust. Working together with other countries around the globe will aid in America's larger struggle to protect itself. As public opinion shows, when America feels threatened, people around the world worry about their own safety and the possible repercussions of U.S. policies. . . .

The United States cannot afford being threatened by terrorists, nor disliked by allies, and uncared for by trading partners and developing countries. It is also in the security interests of the U.S. to convince international publics of its intentions to bring peace and democracy to the world, not act as a global bully or policeman. Doing so weakens America's strategic partnerships and military alliances when potential partners doubt the sincerity of U.S. policies and are skeptical of U.S. motives. The image of America should echo the words of its framers and long-term shapers, the very people that make up American society today. The country was made for everyone. Let's hope it can be seen like that again one day.

2

Poor U.S. Public Diplomacy and Foreign Policies Create Anti-Americanism

Nancy Snow

Nancy Snow is a senior fellow at the Center on Public Diplomacy at the University of Southern California and associate professor of communications at California State University, Fullerton. She is also the author of The Arrogance of American Power.

The U.S. government's recent attempts to counter anti-Americanism are flawed and counterproductive. Its current public diplomacy programs merely promote the United States and its values as a "brand" and even threaten to alienate nations that are historically pro-American, which is troubling given the global opposition against the U.S.-led Iraq war. Moreover, many nations view U.S. foreign policy as widening the gap between rich and poor nations while failing to serve global issues, such as efforts to stop the AIDS epidemic and ethnic and religious violence. As a result, the United States is viewed as an arrogant, self-interested superpower that refuses to listen. To improve its slipping image, the United States must admit to its mistakes, listen during negotiations, and begin to delegate public diplomacy to its citizens.

Anti-Americanism has emerged as a term that, like "fascism" and "communism" in George Orwell's lexicon, has little meaning beyond "something not desirable." However it is

Nancy Snow, "Anti-Americanism and the Rise of Civic Diplomacy," *Foreign Policy in Focus*, December 13, 2006. Reproduced by permission. www.fpif.org/fpiftxt/3795.

defined, anti-Americanism has clearly mushroomed over the last six years, as charted in a number of polls. This phenomenon is, everyone agrees, intimately tied to the exercise of U.S. power and perceptions around the world of U.S. actions.

Neither U.S. global policy nor public diplomacy designed to mitigate its more noxious effects has arrested the steady decline of U.S. popularity in the world.

To counter this anti-Americanism, the U.S. government has embarked on a largely clumsy effort at public diplomacy to convince the world of the benignity of U.S. aims and the universality of U.S. values. Structured like an advertising campaign, this effort has failed to sell the product. Even those who hitherto expressed brand loyalty toward the United States, such as the denizens of "old Europe," have had second thoughts. Neither U.S. global policy nor the public diplomacy designed to mitigate its more noxious effects has arrested the steady decline in U.S. popularity in the world.

It's not too late to rescue public diplomacy. To do so, however, requires a fundamentally different approach. This new strategy must rely more on the ear than the mouth, more on "second track" rather than official diplomacy, and more on civic engagement than the actions of government representatives.

Axis of Anti-Americanism

In September 2006, Venezuela's Hugo Chavez, Iran's Mahmoud Ahmadinejad, and Sudan's Omar Hassan Ahmed Bashir all earned headlines for their harsh and very personal commentary at the UN about all things America. *El Presidente* [George W.] Bush became *El Diablo*, head of the imperialist empire that bullies sovereign states. Chavez and Ahmadinejad claim to represent the people's will by calling out the ubersovereign Bush who terrorizes in his declared war on terror.

The "axis of evil" of Bush's 2002 State of the Union address has been replaced by a more expansive axis of anti-Americanism. This anti-Americanism is the glue that holds together all the third world naysayers who have long opposed what the United States represents culturally, militarily, and economically.

This new axis running through the global South has gained legitimacy thanks to a steep decline in American credibility in the world. The Pew Global Attitudes Project, which has been tracking global public opinion since 2001, indicates that America's image in the world remains consistently negative, particularly as a result of the war in Iraq. The first widely publicized survey released in December 2002 showed that, despite an outpouring of global sympathy after 9/11, the world's superpower fared poorly in image and reputation. The majority in most countries viewed "U.S. policies as contributing to the growing gap between rich and poor nations and believe the United States does not do the right amount to solve global problems." Those problems included the spread of AIDS and other infectious diseases, followed by fear of religious and ethnic violence, and nuclear weapons proliferation. On the precipice of the Iraq War, U.S. leaders should have paid attention to the finding that "the war on terrorism is opposed by majorities in nearly every predominantly Muslim country surveyed."

When asked if he was concerned that his message—that the war on terrorism was not a war on Islam—suffered in translation, the president responded that he hadn't seen the Pew report but that he remained "skeptical" about polls. "I don't run my administration based upon polls and focus groups," Bush said. "I understand the propaganda machines are cranked up in the international community that paints our country in a bad light. We'll do everything we can to remind people that we've never been a nation of conquerors; we're a nation of liberators."

The Pew poll from June 2006 indicates that while anti-Americanism waned somewhat in 2005 due to U.S. aid relief efforts after the Asian tsunami, the U.S.-led war on terror remained a wedge issue not only in the Muslim majority countries but also among U.S. allies like Japan. Majority support for the war on terror exists in just two countries: Russia and India. Majority publics in 10 of the 14 countries surveyed said that the Iraq War was responsible for making the world a more dangerous place. Abu Ghraib [prison in Iraq] and Guantanamo [detention center in Cuba] have received widespread public attention outside the United States, particularly in Western Europe and Japan. Both serve as indicators of America's declining commitment to the rule of law and human rights, making it all the more difficult for America to present itself as the great liberator in Iraq against all those "propaganda machines."

When the United States abdicates its responsibility to uphold the rule of law, human rights, and a free press, then others stand ready to challenge and take up the charge to lead. This is true even if the new leadership, still in the mode of third world dictatorships, is just as oppressive and violating of people's rights.

Defining Anti-Americanism

Barry and Judith Colp Rubin, authors of *Hating America: A History*, define anti-Americanism as systemic antagonism, exaggeration of America's shortcomings for political ends, or mischaracterizations of American society, policies, or goals as ridiculous or malevolent. They make a distinction between opposition, which may be but is not always justified, and anti-Americanism, which they define as illegitimate and extremist:

> Of course, opposition to specific American actions or policies is easily understandable and may well be justifiable, but anti-Americanism as a whole is not. The reason for this conclusion is simply that the United States is not a terrible

or evil society, whatever its shortcomings. It does not seek world domination and its citizens do not take pleasure in deliberately injuring others. There are many occasions when decisions inevitably have drawbacks or bad effects. There are equally many times when mistakes are made. But here is where the line can be drawn between legitimate criticism and anti-Americanism.

There are two problems with this analysis. First of all, it doesn't take into account all the Americans who have challenged U.S. policies. Progress on American policy, whether it is civil rights and civil liberties, protesting the Iraq War, or expanding rights for women and minorities, is often met with fierce resistance. Sometimes opponents use the label "anti-American" to chill this dissent or shut down all debate.

The Rubins' analysis also doesn't acknowledge the real and malign effects of certain U.S. policies as well as U.S. attempts to maintain its unipolar power in the world. Three years before September 11, then-president of the Eurasia Foundation Charles William Maynes criticized the United States for the way it "imperiously imposes trade sanctions that violate international understandings; presumptuously demands national legal protection for its citizens, diplomats, and soldiers who are subject to criminal prosecution, while insisting other states forego that right; and unilaterally dictates its view on UN reforms or the selection of a new secretary general."

Ironically, one of the preemptive techniques of combating anti-Americanism, the association of American values with universal values, has exacerbated rather than solved the problem.

While the events of September 11 did not alter U.S. determination to maintain its global position, global responses to that determination certainly did change. The reaction became more vitriolic and organized at a state and non-state level.

Also, anti-American sentiment was historically reserved for the policies and personalities of a government, but not the people themselves. Especially after the 2004 presidential election, 21st-century anti-Americanism is just as much directed at the American people. As Julia Sweig writes in *Friendly Fire*:

> Americans can no longer take superior comfort from assurances that even our closest historic allies hate us only because of our power and wealth. In addition to the historical, structural, and economic dynamics feeding Anti-America, recent U.S. foreign policy—what we do—has provided a seemingly endless array of inflammatory gaffs that were born not in some madrassa six thousand miles away, nor in a plot hatched by a few neoconservative intellectuals, but of our own society, politics, culture, and actions.

Ironically, one of the preemptive techniques of combating anti-Americanism, the association of American values with universal values, has exacerbated rather than solved the problem. In the past, Tom Paine [influential writer during the American Revolution] made the struggle for American independence part of a global fight for freedom. Today, this assertion of American values as universal comes from an imposing superpower rather than a scrappy underdog.

U.S. promotion of the universality of democratic values like equality, egalitarianism, rule of law, human rights, civil liberties, and freedom are problematic, particularly in the Middle East, which has witnessed three Arab and Muslim country invasions by the United States in the last 14 years. Though it divided opinion in the United States, the Arab street viewed the first Gulf War as mostly acceptable. After all, Iraq had invaded Kuwait, which in turn asked the United States to intervene and kick out the perpetrator. This first invasion of Iraq, which involved many more nations, had the backing of the UN. Even the war in Afghanistan garnered greater worldwide sympathy since it followed an unprovoked attack on the United States and the organizers of the attack were thought to be staging their operation inside Afghanistan.

The war in Iraq, however, has become a deeply divisive policy in the United States and the world. The Middle East population heavily opposes the U.S. presence in Iraq, as do many populations in allied countries of Europe and Japan who think the United States has overstepped its superpower privileges. The Bush Doctrine of preventive war hasn't convinced the global public that the war in Iraq is a just war.

Selling America Abroad

The Department of State remains the chief coordinator of open-sourced U.S. public diplomacy efforts to counter negative attitudes and opinions toward the United States generated by these wars. Most of their efforts are targeting Muslim majority countries of strategic importance to the much maligned war on terror. Since 2001, the State Department has increased funding by 25% to the Near East region, which includes Iran, Iraq, Syria, Lebanon, and Saudi Arabia. [From 2004 to 2006] alone, funding to South Asia (India, Pakistan, and Afghanistan) increased by 39%. These funding levels have not included matching public diplomacy staff levels. Among those staff, a quarter is language-deficient in the areas of concern.

[From 2002 to 2006], the State Department initiated three major public diplomacy activities in the Arabic speaking world. The media campaign "Share Values" ended after [campaign head] Charlotte Beers' departure in 2003. A youth-oriented magazine, *Hi*, was suspended in December 2005. And a series of youth-focused exchange programs also suffered cutbacks due to security concerns and visa problems. Since youth in the Muslim world still remain a primary target, funding for Al Hurra and Radio Sawa broadcasting efforts to the Middle East are continuing. The State Department, along with the Pentagon, the Agency for International Development, and the intelligence agencies are focused on countering global propaganda campaigns of Islamic extremism. President Bush's October 21, 2006 weekly radio address cited the Global Islamic Media Front that is "trying to influence public opinion here in the United States. They have a sophisticated propaganda strategy . . . to divide America and break our will."

This public diplomacy campaign has been less than surefooted. Consider the so-designated "Listening Tour" to the Middle East in September 2005 undertaken by our public diplomacy czar, the former head of domestic campaign spin, Karen Hughes. Al Kamen of the *Washington Post* created his own montage of what newspapers said about the tour. Among the words used to describe the tour were "preachy, culturally insensitive" (*USA Today*), "canned macabre" (*Los Angeles Times*), "lame attempt at bonding" (*Slate*), and "painfully clueless" (*Arab News*).

Before Hughes came on board, her predecessor Charlotte Beers referred to George [W.] Bush and [then–Secretary of State] Colin Powell as the public faces of public diplomacy. Too many references to President Bush, his love of freedom, his man of God position, are counterproductive to marketing a message of "we care" to the rest of the world. The world is at odds with Bush and his policies.

Advice to listen, rather than simply push a product, is central to salvaging the international reputation of the United States.

Beers also described America as the most elegant brand assignment she had undertaken in an advertising career that included packaging Jaguar, Uncle Ben's rice, and many other Fortune 500 brands to the American public and the overseas market. At the time, former Foreign Service Officer John Brown advised America's promoter-in-chief to "remember that America is a country, not a product, and that it can't be 'sold' to the rest of mankind like a brand to be consumed.

Leave marketing to the business sector." He added, "Don't treat foreigners as just potential Republicans. Listen to what they have to say."

Truly Public Diplomacy

This advice to listen, rather than simply push a product, is central to salvaging the international reputation of the United States. John McDonald, a 40-year veteran of the State Department, points to three areas of concern in traditional U.S. international negotiation style and attitude: arrogance, impatience, and lack of listening. The arrogance is a result of a combination of being the world's sole superpower with an over 50-year legacy of American supremacy. Yet American negotiators don't believe that they come across as arrogant, even though McDonald states that "most diplomats from other nations believe that the United States is the most arrogant nation in the world." By bristling at such a characterization and then discounting it altogether, American negotiators only reinforce global perceptions. Americans are also notorious for wanting change to happen almost overnight, when the world seems to operate on a much slower timeline.

The American habit of not listening to global criticism is related to impatience and arrogance. As McDonald characterizes the typical American response, "'Why should we listen carefully?' they ask, 'We already know what is good for you, and we will be pleased to tell you what your needs are and how we can fix those needs.' Because we have not developed good listening skills, which require patience, American diplomats are perceived as superficial, uninterested in other points of view, and therefore arrogant." Even [columnist] Thomas Friedman, the darling of foreign policy opining, urged the Bush administration to show more active listening in diplomacy: "Listening is a sign of respect. It is a sign that you actually value what the other person might have to say. If you just listen to someone first, it is amazing how much they will listen to you back."

But listening is not enough. It is essential to move from the efforts of government officials to those of ordinary people, from the formal world of Track One diplomacy to Track Two diplomacy, in which non-governmental exchanges play a leading role. In September 1996, McDonald led a State Department seminar, "Public Diplomacy and Conflict Resolution: Linking Track One and Track Two Diplomacy." The effort met with a resounding thud. Ten people attended the seminar. Only now is the U.S. government in general and the U.S. State Department in particular beginning to see the need to expand Track Two-style diplomatic efforts.

A promising development was the State Department's creation of a new journalism exchange program. In spring 2006, the new Edward R. Murrow Journalism Program brought 100 foreign journalists to leading journalism schools, including the University of Southern California's Annenberg School for Communication. This program extended ties across multiple sectors, including public, private, and nongovernmental. Partner institutions, however, may keep the journalists tied very closely to on-campus activities and the American public will have limited contact with these VIP journalists. Ideally, though, the journalists will return to their home countries with a balanced, informed, and highly diversified impression of the United States.

The world of diplomacy is no longer hidden from view, and the public diplomat is becoming as much a face of a nation as its appointed secretary of state. Although the State Department is slowly coming around to this understanding, we still need more John McDonald types to educate and train on the second diplomatic track. Public diplomacy is still more about promoting the national security interests of the United States than promoting mutual understanding. This approach still overemphasizes an elite, top-down, official, and formal approach to international relations, with overseas visits that feature handpicked audiences, while underemphasizing the study of what citizens worldwide are doing to prevent conflict and create understanding.

Finally, U.S. officials must be humble enough to admit mistakes. Alberto Fernandez, director of press and public diplomacy for Near Eastern Affairs [in the State Department], told the Arab-language network *Al Jazeera* in a 35-minute interview this last October: "We tried to do our best [in Iraq] but I think there is much room for criticism because, undoubtedly, there was arrogance and there was stupidity from the United States in Iraq." For all of his admirable frankness, Fernandez in short order had to backpedal from his earlier statement and declare a *mea culpa*: "Upon reading the transcript . . . I realized I seriously misspoke by using the phrase 'there has been arrogance and stupidity' by the United States in Iraq. This represents neither my views nor those of the State Department. I apologize." The State Department immediately blamed the error on poor translation, despite the Arabic-language fluency of its senior official.

It is necessary to rescue [U.S.] public diplomacy from official speak.

As an official tasked with bringing more understanding about the United States to the Near Eastern region, Fernandez should be given just a little more elbowroom than usual. After all, he has to explain U.S. policy to a very skeptical public that is more likely to expect propaganda and spin than truth to come out of official Washington. But official Washington cannot see the broader view, which is why it is necessary to rescue public diplomacy from official speak. Get it away from the concentrated control of Washington, DC and into the civic society where people are freer to exchange their views with their overseas counterparts.

Were Fernandez free to speak openly and frankly, he would likely be the best official representative we have on public diplomacy in the Middle East. Because he cannot, we have no choice but to reach out and around the clutches of the State Department and Pentagon to continue to speak the unspun truth one by one, citizen to citizen. The U.S. government is not going to rescue its international reputation without allowing its own citizenry an opportunity to speak on its own terms with people overseas.

3

U.S. Power Creates Anti-Americanism

Soeren Kern

Soeren Kern is senior fellow for transatlantic relations at Grupo de Estudios/Strategic Studies Group, based in Madrid, Spain.

Though the presidential administration of George W. Bush has exacerbated levels of anti-Americanism worldwide, the sentiment is and always has been about American military and economic power. It is by no means a new phenomenon, and feats of American power, such as the Spanish-American War, have long fostered anti-Americanism. In fact, European elites use anti-Americanism in efforts to consolidate Europe into a superpower and seek to counter U.S. military power through laws of the United Nations. Therefore, the only way the United States can appease its international critics is to take measures that reduce its military and economic power, which would compromise its own security.

Bill Clinton has promised that President Hillary [Clinton, 2008 presidential candidate] will dispatch him and George H.W. Bush abroad to repair the supposed damage to our foreign relations allegedly wrought by George W. Bush. Hillary Clinton herself says she would "send a message heard across the world. The era of cowboy diplomacy is over."

How can America improve its image abroad? Answers to this question are being bandied by all of the [2008] presiden-

Soeren Kern, "Anti-Americanism: It's About American Power, Not Policy," *American Thinker*, December 19, 2007. Reproduced by permission of the author. www.american thinker.com/2007/12/antiamericanism_its_about_amer.html.

tial hopefuls. John McCain promises to "immediately close Guantanamo Bay." Ron Paul and Barack Obama both say they would withdraw American troops from Iraq.

Implicit is the notion that George W. Bush has tarnished America's reputation in the world, and that reversing some of his more contentious policies will make the United States popular again. If only it were that simple.

Although polls do indeed show that President Bush has brought anti-Americanism to the surface in many parts of the world, the roots of enmity toward America reach far deeper than one man and his policies. The problem of anti-Americanism will not go away just because Americans elect a new president.

Many Different Brands

Contrary to much of today's conventional wisdom, anti-Americanism is not a recent phenomenon. In Europe, for example, anti-Americanism is as old as the United States itself. In fact, anti-Americanism is so established on the Old Continent that there are now as many different brands of anti-Americanism as there are European countries.

Take Spain, for example, where anti-Americanism goes back to the Spanish-American War, which in 1898 drove the final nail into the coffin of the Spanish empire and ended its colonial exploitation of Cuba. Many Spaniards also resent America's support for General Francisco Franco (1892–1975), who in his day was popular with the Americans because of his strong anti-Communist credentials.

In Germany, anti-Americanism is an exercise in moral relativism. Germans desperately want their country to be perceived as a "normal" country, and its elites are using anti-Americanism as a political tool to absolve themselves and their parents of the crimes of World War II. They routinely equate the US invasion of Iraq with the Holocaust, for example, as a psychological ruse to make themselves feel better about their sordid past.

Indeed, most purveyors of anti-Americanism will continue to bash America until the United States is balanced or replaced . . . as the dominant actor on the global stage.

In France, anti-Americanism is an inferiority complex masquerading as a superiority complex. France is the birthplace of anti-Americanism (the first act of which has been traced to a French lawyer in the late 1700s), and bashing the United States is an inexpensive way to indulge France's fantasies of past greatness and splendor.

As political realists like Thucydides (c 468–395 BC) might have predicted, anti-Americanism is also a visceral reaction against the current distribution of global power. America commands a level of economic, military and cultural influence that leaves many around the world envious, resentful and even angry and afraid. Indeed, most purveyors of anti-Americanism will continue to bash America until the United States is balanced or replaced (by those same anti-Americans, of course) as the dominant actor on the global stage.

In Europe, for example, where self-referential elites are pathologically obsessed with their perceived need to "counterbalance" the United States, anti-Americanism is now the dominant ideology of public life. In fact, it is no coincidence that the spectacular rise in anti-Americanism in Europe has come at precisely the same time that the European Union, which often struggles to speak with one voice, has been trying to make its political weight felt both at home and abroad.

In their quest to transform Europe into a superpower capable of challenging the United States, European elites are using anti-Americanism to forge a new pan-European identity. This artificial post-modern European "citizenship," which demands allegiance to a faceless bureaucratic superstate based in Brussels instead of to the traditional nation-state, is being set up in opposite to the United States. To be "European" means (nothing more and nothing less than) to not be an American.

Because European anti-Americanism has much more to do with European identity politics than with genuine opposition to American foreign policy, European elites do not really want the United States to change. Without the intellectual crutch of anti-Americanism, the new "Europe" would lose its *raison d'être*.

Anti-Americanism also drives Europe's fixation with its diplomatic and economic "soft power" alternative as the elixir for the world's problems. Europeans despise America's military "hard power" because it magnifies the preponderance of US power and influence on the world stage, thereby exposing the fiction behind Europe's superpower pretensions.

Europeans know they will never achieve hard power parity with America, so they want to change the rules of the international game to make soft power the only acceptable superpower standard. Toward this end, European elites seek to delegitimize one of the main pillars of American influence by making it prohibitively costly in the realm of international public opinion for the United States to use its military power in the future. By ensconcing a system of international law based around the United Nations, they hope to constrain American exercise of power. For Europeans, multilateralism is about neutering American hard power, not about solving international problems. It is, as the cliché goes, about Lilliputians tying down Gulliver.

Many American foreign policy mavens refuse to recognize this. In fact, they often over-idolize European soft power, largely because they share the European belief that a multilateral world order is the proper antidote to global anti-Americanism.

Case in point is a new report on "smart power" recently released by the Washington-based Center for Strategic and International Studies (CSIS). The document proffers policy advice based on the fiction that the blame for anti-Americanism lies entirely with the United States. It calls on the next president to fix the problem of anti-Americanism by pursuing a neo-liberal norm-based internationalist foreign policy; it argues, predictably, that America can restore its standing in the world by working through the United Nations and by signing the Kyoto Protocol and the International Criminal Court.

But the report says not a word about the gratuitous anti-American bigotry of Europe's "sophisticated" elites. Nor does it acknowledge that most European purveyors of anti-Americanism are far more opposed to what America *is* than to what America *does*. It is not primarily US foreign policy they seek to change: What Europeans (and many of their American converts) want is a wholesale re-creation of America in the post-modern European pacifist image.

This is the dilemma America faces: If it wants to be popular abroad, it will have to pay in terms of reduced security.

A Zero-Sum Game

To earn the approbation of Europe's sanctimonious elites, the next American president would (for starters) have to relinquish all use of military force, surrender US sovereignty to the United Nations, adopt a socialist economic model, abolish the death penalty, accept an Iranian nuclear bomb, abandon US support for Israel, appease the Islamic world in a high-minded "Alliance of Civilizations". . . and so on.

Anti-Americanism is (at least for the foreseeable future) a zero-sum game because the main purveyors of anti-Americanism are in denial about the dangers facing the world today. They believe the United States is the problem and that their vision for a post-modern socialist multicultural utopia is the answer. Never mind that most Europeans do not have enough faith in their own model to want to pass it on to the next generation.

This is the dilemma America faces: If it wants to be popular abroad, it will have to pay in terms of reduced security. And if it determines to protect the American way of life from global threats, then it will have to pay in terms of reduced popularity abroad.

But if America loses out against the existential threats posed by global terrorism and fundamentalist Islam, then the issue of America's international image will be moot.

Better, therefore, if the next president focuses on keeping America strong and secure, rather than on pleasing those who will never like the United States, even if its foreign policy changes.

Better, also, for the next president to focus on wielding American power wisely, because doing so will earn the United States (grudging) respect, which in the game of unstable relationships that characterizes modern statecraft, is far more important than love.

4

The Prevalence of American Culture Creates Anti-Americanism

Mortimer B. Zuckerman

Mortimer B. Zuckerman is editor-in-chief of U.S. News & World Report.

Anti-Americanism is a reaction to the widespread influence of American culture. From jeans to music to television sitcoms, American popular culture has become a mainstay in virtually every nation in the world and is inextricably linked to popular culture's darker aspects, such as crime, overt sexuality, and materialism. The antiauthoritarian and secular values that the American media project further fuel anti-Americanism. Unfortunately, these much-loathed aspects of American culture overshadow its admirable qualities: individualism, diversity, opportunity, and optimism.

The only things that "every community in the world from Zanzibar to Hamburg recognizes in common" are American cultural artifacts—the jeans and the colas, the movies and the TV sitcoms, the music, and the rhetoric of freedom. That observation was made 65 year ago by Henry Luce in his essay "The American Century," but—to paraphrase President Reagan—Luce hadn't seen anything yet. We have lived through an astounding acceleration in the dissemination of American cul-

Mortimer B. Zuckerman, "What Sets Us Apart," *U.S. News & World Report*, vol. 141, July 3, 2006, p. 72. Copyright © 2006 U.S. News and World Report, L.P. All rights reserved. Reprinted with permission.

tural values with profound implications for the rest of the world. As Plato is widely quoted as having said, "Those who tell the stories rule society."

Our storytellers—encapsulated in the one word: Hollywood—make up a significant piece of America's "soft power." Through the media's projection of the American narrative, the world gets some pretty good insight into America's ideals. Most of the time, since World War II, we have reflected the rule of law, individual freedom, defense of human rights, and the just use of American power against fascism and communism. The American narrative, as portrayed, say, by Jimmy ("aw shucks") Stewart in the Frank Capra classic *It's a Wonderful Life*, enchanted the world.

The message from American pop culture has long been antiauthoritarian, challenging power in ways unthinkable in many countries. The hero, going up against the odds, projected a populist narrative that celebrated the common decencies against the wicked authorities or the excesses of capitalism. Millions who saw such films around the globe derived a sense of phantom citizenship in America, an appetite for the life that only liberty can bring.

The American lifestyle and American capitalism [are] widely viewed as an anarchic revolutionary force.

The universality of the commercial appeal was due in part to Hollywood's munificent creative and marketing skills, but also fundamentally in the fact that we are such a richly heterogeneous society that our exports had been pretested at home. Hollywood supplies over 70 percent of the European film markets and 90 percent of those of the rest of the world, with the possible exception of India. To reach the younger populations under the age of 25, who constitute the bulk of the moviegoing audience, Hollywood has been offering more dumbed-down blockbusters based on action, violence, sex, and special effects like *Jurassic Park*. Such films travel more easily than movies with subtle dialogue or predominantly American references, like *Forrest Gump*. For similar reasons, comedy was structured to hinge on crude slapstick rather than situational wit and wordplay.

The underside of this commercial success is the cultural deficit of associating America with crime, vacuity, moral decay, promiscuity, and pornography—a trend that also worries American parents; Asian and Muslim worlds are already in revolt against it, but also against the libertarian and secular messages of American media. Our media project defiance and ridicule not just of illegitimate authority but of any authority at all—parents, teachers, and political leaders. Even in the West this elicits as much loathing as love. Abroad, it may make dictatorship more difficult, but it also makes democracy less attractive. These images have contributed to make Americanization a dirty word, with the American lifestyle and American capitalism widely viewed as an anarchic revolutionary force. It is perceived as trampling social order in the ruthless pursuit of profits, creating a new class system, based on money, combined with an uninhibited pursuit of pleasure and a disordered sense of priorities in which the needs of the less successful are neglected. What's more, America is increasingly seen as certain of its own righteousness, justifying the use of force to impose American views and values.

So America's narrative, which has waxed for so long, is now waning in its universal appeal. Witness the decline of America's image abroad. In the most recent Pew Research Center poll, favorable opinion of the United States has fallen in most of the 14 countries surveyed, dropping dramatically in Europe, India, and Indonesia, but especially in the Middle East. The main provocation is the war in Iraq. It made anti-Americanism respectable again and crystallized long-standing grievances over American environmental policy and perceived support for globalization, multinational corporations, the death penalty, and friendly authoritarian governments around the world.

These perceptions are badly skewed. They fail to do justice to what is so wonderful about the United States: its individualism, its embrace of diversity, its opportunities for freedom, the welcome it extends to newcomers, and the uniqueness of an entrepreneurial, pragmatic society that is dramatically open to energy and talent. No other country provides the environment for self-help, self-improvement, and self-renovation. No other country possesses our unique mood of buoyancy, optimism, and confidence for the future.

How we portray ourselves positively (while not ignoring the warts) is a challenge to our creative talents—and to all of us.

5

Hollywood Creates
Anti-Americanism

Robert J. Bresler

Robert J. Bresler is editor of national affairs at USA Today, *a publication of the Society for the Advancement of Education, and professor emeritus of public policy at Pennsylvania State University at Harrisburg.*

Since the 1960s, Hollywood movies have portrayed the United States as a nation ruled by a corrupt government and evil multinational corporations, fueling anti-Americanism at home and abroad. From 1979's highly lauded Apocalypse Now *to 2007's blockbuster* The Bourne Ultimatum, *major Hollywood studios inaccurately represent the U.S. military and federal government as ruthless and malevolent and neglect to depict the evils and atrocities America's enemies have committed against the world. Sadly, unlike the patriotic filmmakers of the past, Tinseltown today seems to fear the violent backlash of Muslim insurgents and losing revenues made from international audiences.*

Soon after the bombs dropped on Pearl Harbor [in World War II], Hollywood began making movies to bolster the nation's morale and dramatize its cause. The industry was, as cinematic historian Neil Gabler put it, "turning out film after film about the Nazis' cruelty, the sedition of Nazi sympathizers here, the bravery of our soldiers, the steadfastness of our people and the righteousness of our mission, and they were

Robert J. Bresler, "Hollywood Hates America," *USA Today*, vol. 136, November, 2007, p. 25. Copyright © 2007 Society for the Advancement of Education. Reproduced by permission.

no less zealous against the Japanese" For those of us old enough to have seen those pictures when they first were released, we remember how they reassured us that America eventually would prevail against a sinister enemy in what could be a long and difficult war. Even movies about the darkest days of World War II—such as *Wake Island* (1942) and *Bataan* (1943)—ended on a note of hope and gratitude. Themes of national unity pervaded the culture. Popular music rang out with song after song that unabashedly was patriotic ("He Wears a Pair of Silver Wings," "Praise the Lord and Pass the Ammunition"). Journalists were reluctant to divulge any information that could compromise the war effort or be of value to the enemy. Even the comic strip heroes got into the act as Joe Palooka, Mickey Finn, and Buzz Sawyer joined the military. No doubt Superman and Captain Marvel were involved as well. Certainly, no American film, comic strip, or popular song portrayed our military and its civilian leaders in anything but a favorable light.

Slowly at first, all of that was to change. There were few songs about the Korean War. The few movies that were made about it during the war were forgettable. With the possible exception of Steve Canyon, most of the comic strip heroes stayed home, and it is hard to think of a popular song about that war. One could say that the popular culture was mildly indifferent to the conflict in Asia, but far from hostile.

In the 1960s, the change was far more dramatic. Stanley Kubrick's *Dr. Strangelove or: How I Learned to Stop Worrying and Love the Bomb* (1964) brought a fiercely suspicious attitude toward the military and the whole idea of nuclear deterrence. In that film, the Pentagon command center resembled, as one critic put it, "a tour through a Hollywood insane asylum." The same year, the movie *Seven Days in May* projected a sinister underside to the American military. Burt Lancaster as the chairman of the Joint Chiefs is involved in a plot to overthrow the president who has just signed a nuclear disarmament treaty.

During the Vietnam War, only John Wayne's *The Green Berets* (1968) was an openly pro-American, anti-Vietcong film. The Hollywood establishment was so hostile to Wayne's movie that he had to provide his own financing. Later efforts about Vietnam—such as *Apocalypse Now* (1979), *Platoon* (1986) and *Full Metal Jacket* (1987)—portray the American military effort as hopeless, if not absurd. In the final monologue in *Platoon*, the narrator concludes that, ". . . We did not fight the enemy, we fought ourselves—and the enemy was within us."

Film after film tells of evil at the center of the CIA.

Full-Fledged Paranoia

The Watergate scandal allowed Hollywood to indulge in its full-fledged paranoia about an American government filled with conspirators and sinister schemers. In Oliver Stone's *JFK* (1991) the FBI, CIA, Pentagon, Richard Nixon, and Lyndon Johnson all are implicated in the assassination of John F. Kennedy. From *Three Days of the Condor* (1975) to *The Bourne Ultimatum* (2007), film after film tells of evil at the center of the CIA.

Our victory in the Cold War had little effect upon Hollywood. Despite all we have learned about the Gulag in the Soviet Union, the Stasi in East Germany, the atrocities of [Chinese political and military leader] Mao Tse-Tung's Cultural Revolution, the boat people of Vietnam, the extensive penetration of Soviet agents into the highest reaches of the Roosevelt and Truman administrations, where are the Hollywood movies dramatizing these extraordinary events? For example, where is the film about the Alger Hiss-Whittaker Chambers affair, a story filled with high drama and communist duplicity? Better to produce make-believe films about the CIA or evil multinational corporations.

Did 9/11 change all that? It seems not. The two major cinema works about the incident. *United 93* and *World Trade Center* (both 2006), while admirable, make no mention of Al Qaeda, and we have yet to see a major Hollywood work about the ruthlessness of the jihadists or the bravery of our forces in Iraq and Afghanistan.

What explains this lack of anger and determination in Hollywood against one of the most sinister enemies free people ever have faced? It appears the cynicism and doubt that slipped into American culture during Vietnam and Watergate have not been ameliorated, but rather have metastasized. In *A History of the English-Speaking Peoples Since 1900*, Andrew Roberts writes, "It says much about how far post-Watergate paranoia about the motivations and honesty of public servants had gone that very many people genuinely believed that an American administration and a British government deliberately lied about the level of threat Saddam posed in order to send U.S. and British troops to fight and die in Iraq." Roberts goes on to remind us that such a conspiracy would require the collusion of large numbers of unprincipled people in the highest reaches of government. Michael Moore's *Fahrenheit 911*, which suggests such a thing, won plaudits all over the world.

Is it out of the question for Hollywood to think about making a picture that reminds people of the stakes of this struggle? Are filmmakers so worried that a movie about jihadists would inflame Muslims, as did those Danish cartoons? Are they concerned that any movie extolling the bravery of our forces in Iraq and Afghanistan will not gain the global audience so important to a film's financial success? Is it so much easier to cater to the cynicism and paranoia of the audience than to inspire them? The Hollywood moguls of the 1940s hardly were paragons of virtue, but they look like giants compared to what we have today.

6

Hollywood Does Not Create Anti-Americanism

Robin Bronk

Robin Bronk is executive director of the Creative Coalition, a nonprofit, nonpartisan organization that advocates for the arts and entertainment industry.

Hollywood films and television shows are unjustifiably blamed for fanning the flames of anti-Americanism abroad, just as they are blamed for the United States' problems at home. Hollywood, in fact, takes the heat for the undisputed causes of rising anti-American sentiment, such as the United States' refusal to ratify the Kyoto treaty on global warming and the Iraq war. That Hollywood creates international hit after international hit is a testament to the popularity of its products, not the so-called, over-intellectualized problem of American cultural imperialism.

For some, Hollywood is always to blame. After all, what else but entertainment could possibly cause the breakdown of the American family, teen pregnancy, low test scores, drug use and so many other problems?

Now, though, it seems those looking to make Hollywood the scapegoat have upped the ante. America's brave men and women are fighting wars in Iraq and Afghanistan, the threat of terrorism against Americans looms ever larger and America's reputation around the globe is in free fall. And isn't it obvious to anyone who reads the papers, that this is caused by Hollywood?

Robin Bronk, "Hollywood Has Not Fueled Anti-Americanism Abroad," *ABC News*, December 11, 2006. Copyright © 2006 ABC News Internet Ventures. Reproduced by permission. http://abcnews.go.com/print?id=2717175.

Clearly, we should all be concerned about the rise of anti-American sentiment abroad. Our nation's reputation has taken a beating. . . . From 2000 to this year [2006], the percentage of Germans with a favorable opinion of the United States has dropped from 78 percent to 37 percent. In Britain, we've fallen from 83 percent to 56 percent. In the Muslim world, perhaps unsurprisingly, we're not exactly beloved, with ratings in Indonesia dropping from 75 percent to 30 percent.

When one looks at the results of these surveys done by the Pew Global Attitudes Project, you see tremendous international opposition to the war in Iraq and America's policies on global warming.

If you speak with foreign leaders, you hear genuine concern about specific aspects of U.S. foreign policy: the refusal to agree to the Kyoto Treaty on global warming, the withdrawal from the International Criminal Court, the war in Iraq, difficulty getting visas to visit the United States.

An Easy Explanation

Now, maybe these are just the wrong polls, or we're talking with the wrong foreigners, but I've yet to hear anyone mention Harry Potter as the fuel that feeds the anti-American fire raging across so much of the globe. The over-intellectualized theories of cultural imperialism just defy logic.

Look at Turkey, where our favorability rating has fallen from 52 percent to 12 percent [from 2000 to 2006]. A couple of months back, the No. 1 movie at the Turkish box office was *Garfield: A Tale of Two Kitties.* Rather than face the tough realities of war and international diplomacy, the blame-Hollywood-first crowd argues that our unpopularity in Turkey is the result of an animated cat.

We ought to be grateful for Hollywood's success. Exports of American entertainment are a key engine of our economy. Hollywood has a trade surplus with every other country in the world, something that not many industries can claim.

If we were talking about the auto industry, everyone would hail American ingenuity. But when we talk about movies, the blame-Hollywood-first crowd sees cultural imperialism and an easy explanation for America's waning global popularity.

If American movies bred anti-American sentiment, don't you think Iran and North Korea would have compulsory Sunday matinees?

American media does well internationally for one reason only—we're making a product that people like. We're not forcing anyone to watch. Our product is so popular that some foreign governments, particularly those that oppose America most, restrict their citizens' access to the entertainment of their choice. If American movies bred anti-American sentiment, don't you think Iran and North Korea would have compulsory Sunday matinees?

Of course, some people abroad don't like the prevalence of U.S. media. Is the media driving their anti-Americanism or is their anti-Americanism fueling their fights against U.S.-produced entertainment? The latter explanation makes much more sense.

And what's the alternative? We can refuse to give foreign audiences access to the movies and television they want. That seems to me the ultimate in paternalism and an unacceptable solution. Or we can make films and television shows that are less likely to raise the ire of America's critics abroad.

Is that the answer, to have the mullahs set the bar for what all of us can see? *Baywatch* is a lot less appealing when the lifeguards are wearing burkas.

7

Many Intellectuals Are Anti-American

Paul Johnson

Paul Johnson is a British historian and author. His latest book is Intellectuals: From Marx and Tolstoy to Sartre and Chomsky.

Intellectuals, especially those in Western Europe, are some of the most vicious perpetrators of anti-Americanism. However, it is deeply illogical for them to be anti-American for two major reasons: Intellectuals have benefited greatly from the model of freedom of speech and press that was founded in the United States, and hating the United States is essentially hating humanity, since it is the world's first and largest multiracial society, representing every culture and race in the world. Yet, intellectuals continue to personify their hatred for America in the God-fearing, clear-cut-thinking Texan George W. Bush, who is as American and anti-intellectual as anyone can be.

Anti-Americanism is a phenomenon which, though common and ubiquitous, is difficult to explain because it is illogical, irrational, contradictory, and mysteriously primitive. A good deal of it is parroting. And, oddly enough, a parrot has recently emerged in England which may cast light on the subject. This bird had been owned by a long-distance truck driver who emigrated, bequeathing it to a bird sanctuary. There it behaved well; but there were exceptions. In succession, a local mayor, wearing his chain of office, a police in-

Paul Johnson, "Hating America, Hating Humanity: Yup, That's What They Do—Especially the Intellectuals," *National Review*, vol. 57, September 12, 2005, p. 18. Copyright © 2005 by National Review, Inc., 215 Lexington Avenue, New York, NY 10016. Reproduced by permission.

spector, and a female vicar—all visitors to the sanctuary—were subjected to four-letter verbal abuse. The manager of the place eventually concluded that the parrot had been trained by its owner to abuse authority figures, and recognized them by something distinctive in their dress.

The people among whom anti-Americanism is most rife, who articulate it and set the tone of the venom, are the intellectuals.

The United States, in a lawless and dangerous world where the U.N. cannot impose order—in fact sometimes makes disorder worse—has become a reluctant authority figure, a stepfather or foster parent to a dysfunctional and violent family. As such, it is resented and abused, all the more so since it wears the uniform of its role, the ability to project military power in overwhelming strength almost everywhere in the world. The fact that, in logic, America's critics may be grateful to a nation which, in the past as in the present, has been essential to their liberty and well-being by resisting and overcoming totalitarianism, or suppressing threats to civil society by terrorism, makes no difference to the resentment; may even intensify it.

The people among whom anti-Americanism is most rife, who articulate it and set the tone of the venom, are the intellectuals. They ought logically to hold America in the highest regard, for none depend more completely on the freedom of speech and writing which America upholds, or would suffer more grievously if the enemies against whom America struggles were to triumph and rule or misrule the world. Indeed, many of the most violently anti-American intellectuals benefit directly and personally from America's existence, since their books, plays, music, and other creations enjoy favor on the huge American market, and dollar royalties form a large part of their income. But it is a fact that intellectuals are fundamentally and incorrigibly antinomian. To them, authority, especially if legitimate and benign, is the enemy-in-chief, to be resisted instinctively as a threat to their "freedom," even if such authority ultimately makes it possible. You might think that some of these intellectuals—British, French, German, for instance—who have been particularly abusive of the U.S. would renounce their American royalties. But not one has done so. When I put this point to a leading author, famous alike for his American following and his anti-American views, I was sharply told: "I regard such gestures as childishly quixotic."

Hate America, Hate Humanity

Not only among intellectuals but among a much wider circle, anti-Americanism has a tone of outraged morality which strikes me as peculiarly perverse. It is notable among those, particularly in France, Germany, the Netherlands, and Scandinavia, who profess concern for the well-being of the world (as opposed to the national interest of their countries). These "lovers of humanity" are peculiarly anti-American. Yet what is the United States? It is, so far, the world's only unqualified success in building on the largest possible scale a multiracial society. Every culture in the world is represented in the U.S., usually in considerable numbers. To take in the peoples of the world is not only a U.S. tradition but a current and future reality. Some of the most successful U.S. communities—the Koreans, the Lebanese, the Vietnamese, and the Cubans—are quite recent creations. Immigration from all over our planet is a major factor in pushing America's population over the 300 million mark and, according to the latest projection, will raise U.S. population to 420 million by mid-century. America comes much closer to the realization of world brother-and-sisterhood than that corrupt and soulless abstraction, the United Nations. Indeed the United States is a practical and on the whole prosperous and contented celebration of the essential unity of the planet. To hate America is thus not to hate a particular nation as such, but to hate humanity. And of course it is a melancholy fact that many intellectuals do hate the human race. My definition of an intellectual is someone who thinks ideas matter more than people.

In this confused spasm of irrationality which is anti-Americanism, there is a process of personification which has currently settled on the necessarily lonely figure of George W. Bush. He is much hated among the European intelligentsia, and there are frequent calls for his prosecution as a war criminal, especially among those who took the mass atrocities of a Saddam Hussein or a [communist leader] Pol Pot with equanimity, not to say indifference. And the reason for this is simple, and much to Mr. Bush's credit: To an anti-American, he is the archetype, the quintessential American. He is Mr. America, America personified, even caricatured. He brings out all the envy, fear, and emotional anxiety which lies at the root of the anti-American disease. He is good-looking, upright, a Texan, a man of wealth and self-assurance. He is not by nature talkative, does not articulate abstract thoughts or concern himself with fine distinctions. He sees the world in black-and-white terms, with clear and absolute differences between good and evil, right and wrong. He worships God. He is a Ten Commandments man. He does not meet trouble halfway and is slow to anger, but when roused his anger is terrible and enduring. His personal life centers around the family, an institution European intellectuals view with unease and marked qualifications, not to say distaste. He does not dance effortlessly on the sacramental turf of the campus, or fit into the smoke-filled culture of the basement cafe, or find books axiomatically preferable to the saddle. Does he read poetry to relax, or study philosophy as a hobby, or worship Picasso? No. All this adds up to a terrible indictment.

Mr. Bush enables the more bigoted and inveterate anti-Americans—those for whom anti-Americanism is a culture, almost a way of life—to concentrate their feelings on a real-life actual hate figure. Bush is exactly what the clinical-case anti-American believes the average American is, must be, and, in the weird logic of demonology, ought to be. The Americans elected him. Well, they would, wouldn't they? He is America. Anti-Americanism and Bush hatred are part of the same paranoid emotion. But the obverse is also true. In a difficult time, Bush is America's natural leader.

8

The U.S.'s Position as the Sole Superpower Creates Anti-Americanism

Robert Kagan

Robert Kagan is a senior associate at the Carnegie Endowment for International Peace and transatlantic fellow at the German Marshall Fund. He is also a monthly columnist for the Washington Post.

Although the Iraq war has stoked high levels of anti-Americanism across the globe, it also has rekindled hostilities toward the United States that have deep roots. The position of the United States as a "hyperpower" has angered many countries for many decades. Allegations of American colonialism and destructive military interventions—from Rwanda to Bosnia—are still major points of contention for many world leaders. Therefore, even when the Iraq war ends and George W. Bush leaves office, international resentment may dip, but will remain and peak again. But as the world's only superpower, the United States cannot let the hatred such power brings paralyze it into fearful inaction.

I recently took part in a panel discussion in London about civil conflict and "failed states" around the world, centered on the interesting work of the British economist Paul Collier. The panelists included the son of a famous African liberation-leader-turned-dictator, the former leader of a South American guerrilla group, a Pakistani journalist, a U.N. official and the

Robert Kagan, "Anti-Americanism's Deep Roots," *Washington Post*, June 19, 2006. Reprinted by permission of the author. www.washingtonpost.com/wp-dyn/content/article/2006/06/18/AR2006061800900_pf.html.

head of a nongovernmental humanitarian organization. Naturally, our reasoned and learned discussion quickly transmogrified into an extended round-robin denunciation of American foreign policy.

The interesting thing was that the Iraq war was far from the main topic. George W. Bush hardly came up. The panelists focused instead on a long list of grievances against the United States stretching back over six decades. There was much discussion of the "colonial legacy" and "neo-colonialism," especially in the Middle East and Africa. And even though the colonies in question had been ruled by Europeans, panelists insisted that this colonial past was the source of most of the world's resentment toward the United States. There was much criticism of American policy during the Cold War for imposing evil regimes, causing poverty and suffering throughout the world, and blocking national liberation movements as a service to oil companies and multinational corporations. When the moderator brought up nuclear weapons proliferation and Iran, the panelists talked about Hiroshima and Nagasaki.

America Always at Fault

As for "failed states" and civil conflict, several panelists agreed that they were always and everywhere the fault of the United States. The African insisted that Bosnia and Kosovo were destroyed by American military interventions, not by Slobodan Milosevic, and that Somalia was a failed state because of American policy. The Pakistani insisted the United States was to blame for Afghanistan's descent into anarchy in the 1990s. The former guerrilla leader insisted that most if not all problems in the Western Hemisphere were the product of over a century of American imperialism.

Some of these charges had more merit than others, but even the moderator became exasperated by the general refusal to place any responsibility on the peoples and leaders of countries plagued by civil conflict. Yet the panelists held their ground. When someone pointed out that the young boys fighting in African tribal and ethnic wars could hardly be fighting against American "imperialism," the African dictator's son insisted they were indeed. When the head of the NGO paused from gnashing his teeth at American policy to suggest that perhaps the United States was not to blame for the genocide in Rwanda, the African dictator's son argued that it was, because it had failed to intervene. The United States was to blame both for the suffering it caused and the suffering it did not alleviate.

Deep Roots

The discussion was illuminating, There is no question that the Iraq war has aroused hostility toward the United States around the world. And there are many legitimate criticisms to be made about America's conduct of the war. But it is worth keeping in mind that this anger against the United States also has deep roots.

The Iraq war has rekindled myriad old resentments toward the United States, a thousand different complaints, each one specific to a time and place far removed from the present conflict. It has united a diverse spectrum of anti-American views in common solidarity—the Marxist Africans still angry over American policy in the 1960s and '70s, the Pakistanis still furious at America's (bipartisan) support for the dictator Gen. Mohammed Zia ul-Haq in the 1970s and '80s, the French theoreticians who started railing against the American "hyperpower" in the 1990s, the Latin ex-guerrillas still waging their decades-old struggle against North American imperialism, the Arab activists still angry about 1948 [establishment of Israel as an independent state]. At a conference in the Middle East a few months ago, I heard a moderate Arab scholar complaining bitterly about how American policy had alienated the Arab peoples in recent years. A former [President Bill] Clinton official sitting next to him was nodding vigorously but then suddenly stopped when the Arab scholar made clear that by "recent years" he meant ever since 1967.

The Iraq war has also made anti-Americanism respectable again, as it was during the Cold War but had not been since the demise of the Soviet Union. People who a decade ago would not have been granted a platform to spout the kind of arguments I heard on this panel are now given star treatment in the Western and global media. Such people were always there, but no one was listening to them. Today they dominate the airwaves, and this in turn is helping produce an increasingly hostile global public opinion, as evidenced in a recent Pew poll.

The fact is, because America is the dominant power in the world, it will always attract criticism and be blamed both for what it does and what it does not do.

There are two lessons to be drawn from all this. One is that in time the current tidal wave of anti-Americanism will ebb, just as in the past. Smarter American diplomacy can help, of course, as can success in places such as Iraq. But the other lesson is not to succumb to the illusion that America was beloved until the spring of 2003 and will be beloved again when George W. Bush leaves office. Some folks seem to believe that by returning to the policies of Harry Truman, [former U.S. Secretary of State] Dean Acheson and John F. Kennedy, America will become popular around the world. I like those policies, too, but let's not kid ourselves. They also sparked enormous resentment among millions of peoples in many countries, resentments that are now returning to the fore. The fact is, because America is the dominant power in the world, it will always attract criticism and be blamed both for what it does and what it does not do.

No one should lightly dismiss the current hostility toward the United States. International legitimacy matters. It is important in itself, and it affects others' willingness to work with us. But neither should we be paralyzed by the unavoidable resentments that our power creates. If we refrained from action out of fear that others around the world would be angry with us, then we would never act. And count on it. They'd blame us for that, too.

9

The Hypocrisy of the U.S. Creates Anti-Americanism

Gamil Mattar

Gamil Mattar is director of the Arab Centre for Development and Futuristic Research, based in Cairo, Egypt.

The arrogance of the United States and its superiority complex cause anti-Americanism. But it is the hypocrisy with which the U.S. government acts that truly stirs global hatred. For example, a succession of American presidents have declared war on other countries under the guise of restoring justice, human rights, and individual freedoms. The government's true motive, however, was self-interest. The United States also hypocritically tramples on its own citizens' rights, freedoms, and welfare. Thus, the United States needs to do more than clean up its image: It needs to significantly improve its performance.

[Cuban dictator] Fidel Castro, Washington used to boast, was the only troublemaker in Latin America, a continent of 35 governments, most of them loyal to, and dependant upon, the US. Then along came [Venezuela President] Hugo Chavez and [Bolivia President] Evo Morales to give South America a new injection of vigour, just as US popularity plummeted to an all-time low. Not that Latin America is alone in its sentiments. International public opinion, as gauged in a recent opinion poll conducted by the Pew Global Attitudes Project, which canvassed 91,000 people in 50 nations, found the great majority expressing discontent with America.

Gamil Mattar, "Anti-Americanism Comes of Age," *Al-Ahram Weekly*, June 8–14, 2006. Reproduced by permission. http://weekly.ahram.org.eg/2006/798/op2.htm.

In practical terms, the general tide of global opinion has translated itself into vehement opposition to American interventionism.

How did sentiment toward the US turn so sour? How did the [George W.] Bush administration, in particular, and US policy, in general, manage to turn international opinion pundits into anti-American troublemakers?

In *America Against the World* Andrew Kohut and Bruce Stokes write that a poll they conducted through the Pew Global Attitudes Project reveals that the US, once seen as a bastion of democracy, is now viewed as a warmonger. Seventy per cent of those polled outside the US believe that the world would be safer if another military power emerged to rival the US for global leadership.

Some analysts see the results as a confirmation of Washington's dismal foreign policy performance since the end of the Cold War. Despite the imperialist drive of Republican presidents and the growing militarism of the American state apparatus, they argue, the US has failed to consolidate the bases of its empire or establish an American-led mono-polar system capable of ensuring peace and stability.

Why is it . . . that the American people and press invariably believe the deceptions of their presidents when going to war only to discover later that they have been duped?

The Arrogant Idea

Leftist American historian Howard Zinn has contributed an important insight to the debate. Why is it, he asks, that the American people and press invariably believe the deceptions of their presidents when going to war only to discover later that they have been duped? Zinn attributes the phenomenon to two primary causes; the first involving "the dimension of time", by which he means an absence of historical perspective, the second "the dimension of space", i.e., an inability to think outside the boundaries of nationalism. Americans are "penned in by the arrogant idea" that their country "is the centre of the universe, exceptionally virtuous, admirable, superior." This ethnocentric sense of moral superiority into which Americans have been inculcated by their educational system and their culture makes them particularly vulnerable to government deception. How can the leaders of this great nation go wrong? What they have not been told is that their country's political history is full of presidents who blatantly lied to the American people when they told them they had to go to war to defend their land, democracy and way of life. Moreover, the American people have perpetuated this phenomenon by not correcting their history books, which tell American schoolchildren that in 1846 President Polk declared war against Mexico because Mexico had "shed American blood on American soil" whereas in fact Polk and an elite group of landowners were anxious to get their hands on half of Mexico. In 1898 President McKinley told Americans that his aim in invading Cuba was to liberate it from Spanish rule. The truth was that the United Fruit Company wanted to expel foreigners from the Caribbean so as to eliminate competition. The same president also lied when he sent American forces into the Philippines to "spread civilisation among the savage natives." The motive, again, was purely territorial.

Zinn goes on to list the other instances of presidential whoppers: Truman's justifications for dropping the atom bomb on Hiroshima and Nagasaki; Kennedy's, Johnson's and Nixon's lies for escalating the war in Vietnam, Reagan's reasons for invading Granada and Bush senior's and Bush junior's ostensible grounds for their wars against Iraq. Zinn goes on to argue that if the American people learned "history that is honest about the past" they would cease to allow their presidents to lie to them. He adds that until the American people honestly appraise their history "then we are ready meat for carnivorous politicians and the intellectuals and journalists who supply the carving knives."

What really makes people's gall rise . . . is the arrogance with which the Americans . . . claim to be acting in the name of principles which they are happy to trample underfoot.

Irony of U.S. Principles

This analysis, which appeared in the April edition of *The Progressive*, goes a long way to explaining the worldwide unrest against the US and its policies. What really makes people's gall rise, in Latin America, the Arab and Islamic world, in Britain, Germany, China and Russia, is the arrogance with which the Americans, even at their most diplomatic, claim to be acting in the name of principles which they are happy to trample underfoot. Justice, individual freedoms, minority rights, the rights of the poor—of particular concern to the majority of the world's population, the right of self-determination, the separation between religion and politics, a decent public education system, a reasonably priced healthcare system, the right to a dignified retirement pension—all have been systematically eroded inside the US even before their supposed export abroad. International public opinion is no dope. It knows that one in five children in the US, a country with an $8.3 trillion national debt, is born in poverty, that the WHO ranks the US 37th in terms of the quality of healthcare it provides its citizens and that more than 40 countries have lower infant mortality rates. These facts have become part of the image of America in recent years, along with the way it is pushing its weight around.

During the presidency of George W. Bush political activists and government officials in many countries have become ever more determined to combat Washington's arrogance and are developing ways of doing so. Morales and Chavez did not emerge in a vacuum, and what applies to the two Latin American leaders applies to officials in Iran and Palestine, government leaders in Moscow and Beijing, and the leaders of political parties and mass movements in Germany, Britain, France, Spain, Argentina, Mexico, South Korea, Pakistan and Indonesia. They are all graduates of the same academy of opposition to US policy that Washington has created. And more are on their way. In Addis Ababa the president of Ethiopia recently turned round and criticised the policies of both the US and UK, reserving especially harsh words for [former British] Prime Minister Blair. Apparently the West's friends in Africa are about to form the next wave of anti-American agitators. Recently, I also read reports of an Arab leader, whose government boasts of its close strategic relationship with the US, announcing to his people that the US was punishing his government because "we refuse to toe the line." Here is yet another example of a US ally, whose regime is propped up by American political and financial support, joining the flood of opponents to American policy that are thumbing their noses at the US in order to placate their own people, because they themselves are angry or vengeful, or because it is now the thing to do.

Anti-Americanism comes in varying degrees. It ranges from leaders who rail against US intervention in their national affairs to the leaders of Al-Qaeda and the like who are waging small wars in various parts of the world against the US, its friends and their interests.

Substantive Rather Than Cosmetic

The Shanghai Group, originally formed by China, Russia, Kazakhstan, Uzbekistan, Tajikistan and Kyrgyzstan, is one of the fruits of the American school for producing malcontents. During its first convention the group issued a resolution condemning Washington for attempting to create a military cordon around Russia and China and demanding the departure of US forces from Central Asia. The group is expected to escalate its opposition to US policies in Central and Southern Asia, and has announced that Iran, India, Pakistan and Mongolia will be invited to join the organisation during its next meeting, to be held in Shanghai on the eve of the G8 Summit in St. Petersburg.

The US needs to do more than tidy up its image. It needs a substantive, rather than cosmetic, improvement in its performance. It is incredible, after all the setbacks Washington has encountered abroad, that Washington could remain as arrogant and highhanded toward Arab and Muslim peoples as it was during [Israeli Prime Minister Ehud] Olmert's recent visit, when it insisted that they should mind their own business while the US and Israel, with help from some Arab regimes, puts into effect a new policy of genocide against the Palestinians while simultaneously complaining of troublemakers and extremists.

10

Europe Is Anti-American

Andrei S. Markovits

Andrei S. Markovits is a professor of comparative politics and German studies at the University of Michigan at Ann Arbor. The following viewpoint is adapted from his latest book, Uncouth Nation: Why Europe Dislikes America.

Anti-Americanism runs deep in Europe, historically and as a contemporary phenomenon. In fact, hostility toward the United States is rising and unifies much of Europe—especially its western nations. From the general public to the social elite, Anti-Americanism is accepted as both proper etiquette and academic discourse. Anti-Americanism in Europe also is driven by three factors: America's religious fundamentalism and use of capital punishment, its capitalist mindset, and its cultural inferiority. Therefore, "Americanization" in any form—in the workplace, in the legal system, and even at sports stadiums—is highly resented and discouraged, to the point that anti-Americanism, as a movement, is creating an increasingly aware, assertive, and powerful Europe.

When my father and I arrived in the United States as immigrants from Romania—by way of Vienna—in the summer of 1960, we spent a number of weeks living with American families in the greater New York area. Some were Jews, like us; most were not. But all spoke some German because our English was virtually nonexistent at the time. What

Andrei S. Markovits, "Western Europe's America Problem," *Chronicle Review*, January 19, 2007. Reproduced by permission of the author. http://web.archive.org/web/20070124103109/http://chronicle.com/temp/reprint.php?id=5cm8m89n8bpb099csz9q n8p6z7nzj8xp.

impressed me no end, and will always remain with me, was how all those people adored my Viennese-accented German, how they reveled in it, found it elegant, charming, and above all oh-so-cultured. For business and family reasons, my father had to return to Vienna, where I attended the Theresianische Akademie, one of Austria's leading gymnasia. The welcome accorded to me in that environment was much colder and more distant than it had been in the United States, not by dint of my being a *Tschusch* and a *Zuagraster*, an interloper from the disdained eastern areas of Europe, but by virtue of having become a quasi American.

Any trip to Europe confirms what surveys have been finding: The aversion to America is becoming greater, louder, more determined.

From the get-go until my graduation, many years later, I was always admonished by my English teachers, in their heavily accented, Viennese-inflected English, not to speak this abomination of an "American dialect" or "American slang," and never to use "American spelling," with its simplifications that testified prima facie to the uncultured and simpleton nature of Americans. Of course any of my transgressions, be it chatting in class or playing soccer in the hallways, was met with an admonition of, "Markovits, we are not in the Wild West, we are not in Texas. Behave yourself." Viennese-accented German, wonderful; American-accented English, awful. The pattern still pertains nearly 50 years later.

Any trip to Europe confirms what surveys have been finding: The aversion to America is becoming greater, louder, more determined. It is unifying Western Europeans more than any other political emotion—with the exception of a common hostility toward Israel. Indeed, the virulence in Western Europe's antipathy to Israel cannot be understood without the presence of anti-Americanism and hostility to the United

States. Those two closely related resentments are now considered proper etiquette. They are present in polite company and acceptable in the discourse of the political classes. They constitute common fare not only among Western Europe's cultural and media elites, but also throughout society itself, from London to Athens and from Stockholm to Rome, even if European politicians visiting Washington or European professors at international conferences about anti-Americanism and anti-Semitism are adamant about denying or sugarcoating that reality.

An Anti-American Iceberg

There can be no doubt that many disastrous and irresponsible polices by members of the [George W.] Bush administration, as well as their haughty demeanor and arrogant tone, have contributed massively to this unprecedented vocal animosity on the part of Europeans toward Americans and America. Indeed, they bear responsibility for having created a situation in which anti-Americanism has mutated into a sort of global antinomy, a mutually shared language of opposition to and resistance against the real and perceived ills of modernity that are now inextricably identified with America. I have been traveling back and forth with considerable frequency between the United States and Europe since 1960, and I cannot recall a time like the present, when such a vehement aversion to everything American has been articulated in Europe. No Western European country is exempt from this phenomenon—not a single social class, no age group or profession, nor either gender. But the aversion reaches much deeper and wider than the frequently evoked "anti-Bushism." I perceive this virulent, Europewide, and global "anti-Bushism" as the glaring tip of a massive anti-American iceberg.

Anti-Americanism has been promoted to the status of Western Europe's lingua franca. Even at the height of the Vietnam War, in the late 1960s and early 1970s, and during the dispute over NATO's Dual Track decision (to station Pershing and cruise missiles primarily in Germany, but in other Western European countries as well, while negotiating with the Soviet Union over arms reduction), things were different. Each event met with a European public that was divided concerning its position toward America: In addition to those who reacted with opposition and protest, there were strong forces that expressed appreciation and understanding. In France, arguably Europe's leader over the past 15 years in most matters related to antipathy toward America, the prospect of stationing U.S. medium-range missiles, especially if they were on German soil, even met with the massive approval of the left in the late 1970s and early 1980s.

But as of October 2001, weeks after 9/11 and just before the U.S. war against the Taliban regime in Afghanistan, a massive Europewide resentment of America commenced that reached well beyond American policies, American politics, and the American government, proliferating in virtually all segments of Western European publics. From grandmothers who vote for the archconservative Bavarian Christian Social Union to 30-year-old socialist Pasok activists in Greece, from Finnish Social Democrats to French Gaullists, from globalization opponents to business managers—all are joining in the ever louder chorus of anti-Americanism.

Ambivalence, antipathy, and resentment toward and about the United States have made up an important component of European culture since the American Revolution.

The Bush administration's policies have catapulted global and Western European anti-Americanism into overdrive. But to understand that overdrive, we need to analyze the conditions under which this kind of shift into high gear could occur. Western Europeans' unconditional rejection of and legitimate outrage over abusive and irresponsible American policies—not to mention massive human-rights violations à la Abu Ghraib, Guantánamo, secret CIA cells—rest on a substantial sediment of hatred toward, disdain for, and resentment of America that has a long tradition in Europe and has flourished apart from those or any other policies.

Ambivalence, antipathy, and resentment toward and about the United States have made up an important component of European culture since the American Revolution, thus way before America became the world's "Mr. Big"—the proverbial 800-pound gorilla—and a credible rival to Europe's main powers, particularly Britain and France. In recent years, following the end of the cold war, and particularly after 9/11, ambivalence in some quarters has given way to unambiguous hostility. Animosity toward the United States has migrated from the periphery and become a respectable part of the European mainstream.

Negative sentiments and views have been driven not only—or even primarily—by what the United States *does*, but rather by an animus against what Europeans have believed that America is. While the politics, style, and discourse of the Bush terms—and of President Bush as a person—have undoubtedly exacerbated anti-American sentiment among Europeans and fostered a heretofore unmatched degree of unity between elite and mass opinion in Europe, they are not anti-Americanism's cause. Indeed, a change to a center-left administration in Washington, led by a Democratic president, would not bring about its abatement, let alone its disappearance.

The Dimension of Power

Anti-Americanism constitutes a particular prejudice that renders it not only acceptable but indeed commendable in the context of an otherwise welcome discourse that favors the weak. Just as in the case of any prejudice, anti-Americanism also says much more about those who hold it than about the object of its ire and contempt. But where it differs markedly from "classical" prejudices—such as anti-Semitism, homophobia, misogyny, and racism—is in the dimension of power. Jews, gays and lesbians, women, and ethnic minorities rarely if ever have any actual power in or over the majority populations or the dominant gender of most countries. However, the real, existing United States does have considerable power, which has increasingly assumed a global dimension since the end of the 19th century, and which has, according to many scholarly analyses, become unparalleled in human history.

While other public prejudices, particularly against the weak, have—in a fine testimony to progress and tolerance over the past 40 years—become largely illegitimate in the public discourse of most advanced industrial democracies (the massive change in the accepted language over the past three decades in those societies about women, gays, the physically challenged, minorities of all kinds, and animals, to name but a few, has been nothing short of fundamental), nothing of the sort pertains to the perceived and the actually strong. Thus anti-Americanism not only remains acceptable in many circles but has even become commendable, a badge of honor, and perhaps one of the most distinct icons of what it means to be a progressive these days.

So, too, with hostility to Israel. Because of its association with the United States, Israel is perceived by its European critics as powerful, with both countries seen as mere extensions of one another. To be sure, there is something else at work here as well, because America has many other powerful allies that never receive anywhere near the hostile scrutiny that Israel confronts on a daily basis. Clearly, the fact that Israel is primarily a Jewish state, combined with Europe's deeply problematic and unresolved history with Jews, plays a central role in European anti-Semitism. But today we are witnessing a "new" anti-Semitism that adds to traditional stereotypes: It is an epiphenomenon of anti-Americanism.

The Swiss legal theorist Gret Haller has written extensively to a very receptive and wide audience about America's being fundamentally—and irreconcilably—different from (and, of course, inferior to) Europe from the very founding of the American republic. To Haller, the manner in which the relationships among state, society, law, and religion were constructed and construed in America are so markedly contrary to its European counterpart that any bridge or reconciliation between those two profoundly different views of life is neither possible nor desirable. Hence Europe should draw a clear line that separates it decisively from America. In a discussion with panelists and audience members at a conference on European anti-Americanism at the Diplomatic Academy of Vienna, on April 29, 2005, at which I shared the podium with Haller, she explicitly and repeatedly emphasized that Britain had always belonged to Europe, and that the clear demarcation was never to run along the channel separating Britain from the European continent, but across the ever-widening Atlantic that rightly divided a Britain-encompassing Europe from an America that from the start featured many more differences from than similarities to Europe. The past few years have merely served to render those differences clearer and to highlight their irreconcilable nature.

That widely voiced indictment accuses America of being retrograde on three levels: moral (America's being the purveyor of the death penalty and of religious fundamentalism, as opposed to Europe's having abolished the death penalty and adhering to an enlightened secularism); social (America's being the bastion of unbridled "predatory capitalism," to use the words of former German Chancellor Helmut Schmidt, and of punishment, as opposed to Europe as the home of the considerate welfare state and of rehabilitation); and cultural (America the commodified, Europe the refined; America the prudish and prurient, Europe the savvy and wise).

Defective Democracies

Indeed, in an interesting debate in Germany about so-called defective democracies, the United States seems to lead the way. Without a substantial "social" component, a democracy's defects are so severe that one might as well consider labeling such a system nondemocratic, or at best defectively democratic. To be sure, no serious observer of the United States would dispute the considerable defectiveness of its political system. But what matters in this context is not so much the often appropriate indictment of American democracy, but the total silence about the defects of German and (Western) European democracy. As Klaus Faber, one of this argument's major progressive critics, has correctly countered, surely most segregated and alienated immigrants in the suburbs of Paris or the dreary streets of Berlin would be less likely than America's critics to extol German and French democracies as free of any defects. Indeed, if one extends the "social" dimension to include the successful integration of immigrants, surely America's democracy would emerge as much less defective than the alleged models of Western Europe.

Many of the components of European anti-Americanism have been alive and well in Europe's intellectual discourse since the late 18th century. The tropes about Americans' alleged venality, mediocrity, uncouthness, lack of culture, and above all inauthenticity have been integral and ubiquitous to European elite opinion for well over 200 years. But a bevy of examples from all walks of life highlights how pervasive and quotidian anti-Americanism has become. I have collected my examples from outside of what one would conventionally associate with politics *precisely* to demonstrate that the European animus against things American has little to do with the policies of the Bush administration—or any other administration, for that matter—and is alive and well in realms that have few connections to politics.

Let us turn to language: In German, the terms *Amerika-niesierung* (Americanization) and *amerikanische Verhältnisse* or *amerikanische Bedingungen* (American conditions) almost invariably refer to something at once negative and threatening—something to be avoided. Thus, for example, the Junge Union (the youth branch of the conservative Christian Democratic Union) derided the Social Democratic Party's attempts to introduce primaries on the American model, insisting that German politics needed democratization, not Americanization. The union equated the former with competence in problem solving, the latter with blowing bubbles in the air. For its part, the left has made "Americanization" a pejorative staple of its vocabulary. In Britain, "Americanisation" and "American-style" also have an almost exclusively negative connotation—often with the adjective "creeping" as a telling modifier in front: the creeping Americanization of the car's feel for the road, the cult of guns fueled by creeping Americanization through violent films, the creeping Americanization of the growing girth of British novels, the creeping Americanization of British sport.

Indeed, it seems as if the British find every aspect of the sporting world's Americanization fearful. Thus, for example, *The Guardian* reported complaints in 1995 that British stadiums have increasingly come to resemble those in America and are now equipped with good seats, restaurants, and even dance floors: Abolishing those infamous standing-room sections, or "terraces," where nearly 100 people lost their lives in riots at Hillsborough in Sheffield, has made the sport too "nice." In 1998 *The Independent* intoned: "The creeping Americanisation of British sports, in terms of ubiquitous coverage and potential for earning, means that niceness is at a higher premium than ever before." Americanization has also been blamed for taming fans, who previously cared passionately about whatever game they were watching; now they allegedly attend events primarily to see and be seen.

The Case of Soccer

The world of soccer offers a fine example of my point because, whatever one wants to argue about this sport and its
culture, it is clear that the United States was at best an also-
ran in it throughout the 20th century. America simply did not
matter—and still matters very little—in the world of soccer. It
was never a threat to Europe; or, to put the point in the right
style, America was never a "player." Nevertheless, the discourse
about this game on the European side has always had a cynical, aggressive, irritating, and above all condescending tone.

---

*The concept "Americanization" also connotes ... every
kind of deterioration in the European world of work.*

When the United States was chosen as host of the World
Cup for the summer of 1994, many of the European news and
entertainment media were appalled. Instead of rejoicing that
the last important *terra incognita* for soccer was about to be
conquered by the "beautiful game," Europeans loudly voiced
the usual objections to American crassness, vulgarity, com-
mercialism, and ignorance. They argued that giving the tournament to the Americans was tantamount to degrading the
game and its tradition. Awarding Americans the World Cup
was like holding a world championship in skiing in a country
in the Sahara or playing a major golf tournament in Green-
land—an anomaly bordering on impudence, cheekiness, and
inauthenticity, since, in the European view, the environment
wasn't suited to the sport. The facilities were denigrated, the
organization ridiculed, the whole endeavor treated with deri-
sion. When the stadiums were filled like in no other World
Cup tournament before or since, when the level of violence
and arrests was far and away the lowest at any event that size,
the European media chalked it up to the stupidity and igno-

rance of Americans. Of course Americans came to the games because they like events and pageantry, but did they really enjoy and understand the sport?

The concept "Americanization" also connotes, to give another example, every kind of deterioration in the European world of work—stress through job insecurity, disqualification through work intensification, "flexibility," "mobility"—and is a synonym for all things negative in the very complex entity of a rapidly changing capitalism. People criticize an alleged decline in workmanship and quality of European products, for which they blame the increased competition that Americanization exacts. And the quantity of work is constantly expanding, particularly for managers and others in leading positions. The oxymoron "working vacation" has entered the European vernacular, which again testifies to an Americanization of Europe's work life. Yet rarely, if ever, have I read anything about a purported "Japanization" or—of increasing relevance—"Chinazation" of European work life.

Or consider European discussions of higher education. When, in an article about the American higher-education system that I wrote for the magazine *Spiegel Spezial*, I praised the seriousness with which teaching is viewed in America and also (in contrast to the situation in Germany) evaluated by students, I received numerous letters of protest from my German colleagues. "We are not, thank God, in America, where universities are just upgraded [secondary] schools," wrote one furious correspondent. That students might be allowed to evaluate their professors' teaching was rejected by almost all of my German colleagues as a bad American habit that commercialized the university and damaged professorial and scholarly autonomy. The late conservative Cologne sociologist Erwin K. Scheuch, spokesman for the equally conservative *Bund Freiheit der Wissneschaft* (Federation for Academic Freedom, founded in 1970), had been warning against Americanization in German universities for some time. In a 2002 lecture, "Model

America," he argued that only some 50 institutions of higher education in America deserve the term "university." He went on to call for blocking any attempt to introduce American course credits to German institutions, and decried the introduction of performance-oriented salaries, which he said would destroy Germany's "collegial structures."

Across the Channel, in a 1994 article in *The Guardian*, the journalist Peter Kingston wrote, "Bubblegum University's funny ways are becoming familiar in colleges over here. The huge range and exotic combinations of courses, the spoon-feeding mode of classroom teaching, the obsession with grades, the general acceptance that many students have to take jobs through college," he wrote, "these have become standard features of universitas Britannica." Note: Bubblegum University goes with the purported lowering of traditional standards. It can hardly get more stigmatizing than that.

The Americanization of many aspects of the legal worlds and the administration of justice in Europe also raises anxiety.

Succumbing to American Influence

It is only to be expected that European conservatives would make fun of American feminism, multiculturalism, affirmative action, and the related reform movements that are allegedly ruling the best universities in the United States. There is a bevy of material that mocks such reforms under the rubric of "political correctness." Damned if you do, damned if you don't. While Europeans, as a rule, have complained about the arrogance and elitism of American universities, now they are reproaching them for the exact opposite: that their achievements are being destroyed by the unqualified in the name of political correctness. However, Europe's left-wing liberals have just as much trouble tolerating the themes that are part of that complex. While the thrust of their criticism is different, the tenor is surprisingly similar. During the Clinton-Lewinsky crisis, many European leftists regarded the critical position of some American feminists toward Clinton as laughable. Of course puritanism was (again) to blame.

The Americanization of many aspects of the legal worlds and the administration of justice in Europe also raises anxiety. At an informal meeting with trade unionists in 2002, Germany's former Justice Minister Hertha Däubler-Gmelin claimed that America has a *lausiges* or "lousy" legal system. That view is widely shared in European intellectual circles. There is also a disparaging of America's "claims mentality" and the rapacious litigiousness thought to accompany it. The possibility of introducing courtroom television broadcasts into Germany is seen as succumbing to "American conditions." In Britain, the perceived menace is wide-ranging: ever-larger law firms, higher fees for top-flight attorneys, an epidemic of lawsuits, the proliferation of special courts as part of a doubtful "therapeutic justice" all are creeping and creepy.

European holidays are allegedly increasingly Americanized, with Santa Claus displacing the Virgin Mary and Baby Jesus at Christmas, with the semi-pagan Halloween becoming more prominent, and with birthday celebrations supplanting "name day" ceremonies of yore. Even the wildlife is said to be succumbing to America's influence: In Hamburg and Vienna, there is a growing resentment that predatory black squirrels, brought to Europe from America, are displacing their indigenous, more peaceful cousins.

All of these "Americanizations" bemoan an alleged loss of purity and authenticity for Europeans at the hands of a threatening and unwelcome intruder who—to make matters worse—exhibits a flaring cultural inferiority. America is resented for everything and its opposite: It is at once too prurient and too puritanical; too elitist, yet also too egalitarian; too chaotic, but also too rigid; too secular and too religious; too radical and too conservative. Again, damned if you do, damned if you don't.

The future of anti-Americanism in Europe's public discourse will remain deeply tied to the fate of Europe's unification process, one of the most ambitious political projects anywhere in the world. Fundamentally, the European views about America have little to do with the real America but much to do with Europe. Europe's anti-Americanism has become an essential ingredient in—perhaps even a key mobilizing agent for—the inevitable formation of a common European identity, which I have always longed for and continue to support vigorously, although I would have preferred to witness a different agency in its creation. Anti-Americanism has already commenced to forge a concrete, emotionally experienced—as opposed to intellectually constructed—European identity, in which Swedes and Greeks, Finns and Italians are helped to experience their still-frail emotive commonality not as "anti-Americans" but as Europeans, which at this stage constitutes one sole thing: that they are "non-Americans."

By cultivating an anti-American position, Europe feigns membership in a global opposition of the downtrodden by America.

"Europeanism"

Anti-Americanism will serve as a useful mobilizing agent to create awareness in Europe for that continent's new role as a growing power bloc in explicit contrast to and keen competition with the United States, not only among Europeans but also around the globe. Anti-Americanism has already begun to help create a unified European voice in global politics and will continue to be of fine service to Europe's growing power in a new global constellation of forces, in which an increasingly assertive Europe will join an equally assertive China to challenge the United States on every issue that it possibly can.

For the time being, there seem to be no visible incentives for Europeans to desist from anti-Americanism. Its tone is popular among European publics. Far from harming Europe and its interests, anti-Americanism has helped Europeans gain respect, affection, and—most important—political clout in the rest of the world. Anti-Americanism has become a European currency whose value fluctuates greatly, but whose existence does represent a chip that Europe will cash in with increasing gusto. By cultivating an anti-American position, Europe feigns membership in a global opposition of the downtrodden by America.

It is completely unclear which direction and what kind of political and symbolic content this waving of the European flag will assume: a negative, exclusionary, and therefore arrogant identity formation that [late German-American political philosopher] Hannah Arendt labeled "Europeanism," or a positive and universalistic ideology that builds on the commonalities of Western values and then forms the basis for further European state and nation building. But there can be no doubt about one thing: Outfitted with a mass base and a congruence between elite and mass opinion, anti-Americanism could, for the first time in its long European history, become a powerful political force going well beyond the ambivalences, antipathies, and resentments that have continuously shaped the intellectual life of Europe since July 5, 1776.

11

Europe Is Not Anti-American

Jonathan Rauch

Jonathan Rauch is a guest scholar at the Brookings Institution, a nonprofit political think tank, and a correspondent for The Atlantic Monthly.

Although recent polls show that the international reputation of the United States has slipped in the last decade, emerging European leaders, on the contrary, are pro-American. Unpopular foreign policy alone does not polarize nations; rather, shared interests determine alliances. And the United States and Europe share the same general concerns, such as preventing Iran from acquiring nuclear weapons. Europe's current hostility toward the United States has been caused by Republican George W. Bush's presidential administration, and anti-Americanism will level off there when European-favored Democrats return to power.

Over coffee not long ago, a European diplomat, then completing his five-year tour in Washington, reflected on anti-Americanism. No, he said, it is nothing new. The European left, in particular, has indulged in it for years. But today? Today, he sighed, is different. Since the Iraq War, mistrust of America has penetrated further into the mainstream. It has found lodging with the man in the street.

Polls bear him out. "America's global image has again slipped," began the summary of a fifteen-nation survey by the Pew Global Attitudes Project, in June [2006]. September [2006]

Jonathan Rauch, "Coalition of the Waiting: The U.S.-European Alliance Is Not on Its Last Legs—and When Bush Goes, It Could Emerge Stronger Than Ever," *Atlantic Monthly*, vol. 298, December, 2006, pp. 29–31. Copyright © 2006 *The Atlantic Monthly*. Reproduced by permission.

brought more of the same, this time from the German Marshall Fund of the United States, whose Transatlantic Trends poll surveyed the United States and twelve European countries. The proportion of Europeans "who view U.S. leadership in world affairs as desirable has reversed since 2002," reported the survey, "from 64 percent positive to 37 percent this year, and from 31 percent negative to 57 percent." What about Europe's views of President Bush? Don't ask. Well, all right: for the morbidly curious, his approval rating in Europe is a bottom-scraping 18 percent.

"Atlanticism" as foreign-policy experts often call the idea of a robust U.S.-European partnership, is no kiss of death in European politics.

Surprisingly Pro-American

Yet here is something odd. Such overwhelmingly anti-U.S. sentiment, one might think, should translate into anti-U.S. politics. But it has not. A new generation of European leaders is moving into position, and it is surprisingly pro-American. Angela Merkel, the chancellor of Germany, has gone out of her way to restore transatlantic ties and to call for a strong United States-Europe partnership. From an American point of view, she is a big improvement over her predecessor, Gerhard Schroder.

Tony Blair, the exiting British prime minister, is as solidly pro-American as they come, to the point of being ridiculed as an American lackey. Gordon Brown, Blair's longtime heir apparent, was under pressure to distinguish himself from "Bush's poodle" as he pitched his leadership to the Labour Party in September [2006]. Yet he pointedly staked Labour's renewal "on that essential truth—the need for global cooperation in the fight against terrorism, never anti-Americanism." The glamorously next-gen leader of the British Conservative Party, David Cameron, gave a big foreign-policy speech declaring anti-Americanism "an intellectual and moral surrender," and pronouncing himself and his party "instinctive friends of America and passionate supporters of the Atlantic alliance."

No European leader has been a sharper thorn in the Bush administration's side than France's president, Jacques Chirac, and no country's chattering class has spoken as openly of making Europe a counterbalance to American influence. Yet Nicolas Sarkozy, Chirac's interior minister and the man whom many consider most likely to succeed him, chose, as the *Washington Post* put it, to "kick off the campaign season in France by making a U.S. tour," and by delivering, in Washington, an "unabashedly pro-American speech." He called America "Europe's obvious and natural partner," described the transatlantic bond as "unique and irreplaceable," and in case anyone missed the point, added, "My dedication to our relationship with America is well-known and has earned me substantial criticism in France." Not enough criticism, apparently, to make him sing an anti-American tune.

European voters presumably choose leaders for much more than their posture toward the United States. At the very least, however, it seems clear that "Atlanticism" as foreign-policy experts often call the idea of a robust U.S.-European partnership, is no kiss of death in European politics, and may indeed be a plus. Certainly some very prominent and savvy politicians are betting on it.

The polls point one way, the politics another. Why? The German Marshall Fund's survey suggested an answer. In foreign policy, popularity (or lack of it, in America's case) does not, by itself, determine polarity. Interest trumps it. And, to a surprising extent, the broad publics of America and Europe view their interests the same way.

Both publics share an overwhelming consensus that international terrorism, Islamic fundamentalism, the prospect of a nuclear-armed Iran, and "violence and instability in Iraq" are important threats. Europe is a degree less alarmed about security than the United States, but the two publics share the same general worries and priorities. Both publics believe the European Union should "exert strong leadership in world affairs." Both believe NATO [the North Atlantic Treaty Organization] is essential and view the United Nations favorably. Both agree that economic power is more important than military power. Both agree, overwhelmingly, that "when our country acts on a national security issue, it is critical that we do so together with our closest allies." (A surprise: Americans are more sold on multilateralism than are Europeans.)

Both publics, by almost five-to-one majorities, want to prevent Iran from getting nuclear weapons. They also share a marked reluctance to use military force to that end. But pluralities on both sides favor force if nonmilitary means fail to thwart Tehran's nuclear ambitions. In fact, Europeans are more hawkish on Iran than are American Democrats.

Those numbers suggest a strong U.S.-European affinity— perhaps, indeed, stronger than ever. What, then, gives rise to the unpopularity of America in Europe? Why is it that, as the German Marshall Fund poll finds, Americans want closer transatlantic ties and embrace European leadership, whereas Europeans want more independence from America and mistrust U.S. leadership?

One reason, of course, is the Iraq War, which caused a European crisis of confidence in America's leadership. Another reason is George W. Bush, whom Europeans have made up their minds to loathe. A more enduring difference is Europe's pacifist streak. Europeans and Americans agree that, as a practical matter, military force may eventually be needed to cope with Iran, but they disagree on whether, as a matter of principle, war is ever "necessary to obtain justice" with Europeans taking the dovish side. Europeans' belief that there is no such thing as a good war will make them more reluctant than Americans to pull the trigger in a confrontation with, say, Iran.

Scrubbing the numbers suggests one more reason, perhaps the most intriguing: European opinion has much more in common with the views of U.S. Democrats and independents than with Republicans. For example, most Europeans, U.S. Democrats and U.S. political independents oppose using military force to remove authoritarian regimes, but a majority of Republicans favor it. Substantial majorities of Europeans and U.S. Democrats and independents view the UN favorably, but Republicans take a dim view of it. In some respects, the wider divide is across the partisan aisle, not across the Atlantic Ocean.

Republican partisans ("Bush's base" in the political jargon) have single-handedly run the U.S. government [since 2002]. For better or worse, one-party rule in America placed in charge the U.S faction—a minority of the population, and at best a razor-thin majority of the electorate—that has no counterpart in Europe's political mainstream.

It may turn out, then, that Europe has soured on American leadership for many years to come. That would not paralyze the alliance (and has not), but it would raise the frictional costs of doing routine transatlantic business on everything from NATO to trade, and it would increase the odds of dangerous ruptures in times of confrontation with outside threats or adversaries: Iran most obviously, but also, potentially, China, Russia, [Palestinian Islamist organization] Hamas or [Lebanon-based Islamic organization] Hezbollah, or even—heaven forbid—al-Qaeda itself.

But it is also possible that the elements of a renewed transatlantic alliance—centrist majorities, shared priorities, likeminded leaders—are already falling into place, waiting to be activated by a United States governed from the center of the country, rather than from the center of the Republican Party. To borrow [American political commentator] Robert Kagan's evocative metaphor, Europe's left is from Venus and America's right is from Mars, but perhaps Earth is in sight.

12

Islamic Militants Hate the U.S. Because of Its Freedom

Joseph Loconte

Joseph Loconte is a senior fellow at the Ethics and Public Policy Center and a monthly commentator on religion for National Public Radio. Loconte is also editor of The End of Illusions: Religious Leaders Confront Hitler's Gathering Storm.

Many critics of the United States attribute the anti-American views of Islamic militants to U.S. foreign policy, especially the Iraq war. However, anti-Americanism in the Islamic world is a more fundamental problem—it is closely tied to the democratic ideals, freedoms, and rights that the United States was founded upon and has vowed to protect. Some Muslim intellectuals even link the lack of freedom to economic failure and political strife in Arab nations, where extremist Islamic laws severely restrict speech, free choice, and other human rights. Such beliefs blind them to charity and faith in the noble, decent, and humane and fuel their hatred of what America stands for.

[In September 2007] we learned of another "massive" terrorist plot against American targets, this time thwarted by German authorities, Osama bin Laden has just released another cryptic video threat against the United States, and . . . years since the events of 9/11, still we ask: why do they hate us?

Critics of U.S. foreign policy can cite many reasons for Islamist rage. But they overlook a more fundamental problem:

To al Qaeda and its sympathizers, nothing is more deserving of contempt than the idea of faith as a free and rational choice—a concept more integral to American identity than any other Western democracy.

When Osama bin Laden excoriates the United States as "the worst civilization witnessed by the history of mankind," he has more than America's foreign policy in mind. To violent theocrats, it is not merely the content of contested doctrines that is offensive—it is their very existence. The United States, historically a nation of religious dissenters, is especially odious for this very reason.

Indeed, to the theocrats America's religious diversity is not just staggering but maddening: a Tower of Babel that has turned its spiritual infidelity into an art form. Even Mohammad Khatami, the former Iranian president hailed as a moderate, complains bitterly that Americans "try to disguise their crimes" with seductive rhetoric—the language of freedom, human rights, and pluralism.

Thus, Islamic extremists decry the spiritual corruption of the American "Crusaders" and vow a holy war reminiscent of Saladin's siege of Jerusalem, circa 1187. It does not occur to them that no Western nation has more emphatically rejected Medieval Christendom, with its faith-based repression and hypocrisy, than the United States. By keeping government out of the sanctuary—and priestcraft out of government—the U.S. Constitution has helped protect the integrity of all faith traditions.

America's founders warned repeatedly of the "superstition, bigotry and persecution" generated by state-sanctioned religion. But they were not secularists, nor were they cynical about religious belief. Rather, they viewed "soul liberty" as a natural right—and a spiritual obligation. "It is unalienable also," argued James Madison, "because what is here a right towards men, is a duty towards the Creator." Their great accomplishment was convincing establishment elites that religious pluralism could nurture political and economic prosperity, just as intolerance guaranteed decline.

Deep Wells of Anti-Americanism

Compare these religious ideals to those held by numerous Muslim states—including Egypt, Iran, Pakistan, Saudi Arabia, and Sudan—with deep wells of anti-Americanism. All sustain a political culture that regards non-Muslims with dark suspicion. All have enshrined some version of Shari'a law, which criminalizes or severely restricts speech, worship, and free association of religious minorities. All have spawned terrorist activity against the United States and her allies. And all struggle with massive economic disparities and civic unrest.

Some Islamic leaders are slowly awakening to the problem. A few years ago a group of Muslim intellectuals and scholars, in a remarkable series of U.N.-sponsored reports, explored the causes of economic backwardness and political turmoil in the Arab world. They identified "an acute deficit of freedom" as the core problem. They even argued that Islamic governments should "protect the right of people and groups not only to worship as they wish, in private; but also to promote their values publicly in civil society."

But even these voices of moderation failed to endorse a robust doctrine of religious freedom. They have yet to grasp the quiet genius of the American experiment: the transformative and creative power of faith freely chosen. If authentic belief engages the mind as well as the heart, then the best human faculties—empathy, humility, reason, and conscience—must be summoned in its pursuit.

We must not forget, however, that the road to religious liberty in the West was long and arduous. When, in the 1680s, [English philosopher] John Locke published his bracing defense of religious freedom, "A Letter Concerning Toleration," the political and religious establishment went ballistic. For Locke, neither church nor state could compel belief because faith demanded the "inward and full persuasion of the mind." But Anglican ministers, like their Catholic counterparts, viewed freedom of conscience as a subversive heresy, a license for libertinism. They hounded Locke—and thousands of dissenters like him—as a "locust from the pit of hell."

Why do they hate us? For some of the same reasons an earlier generation of Pharisees [or religious separatists] despised Locke. Their religion has become a cloak for their lust to dominate "No man can be a Christian without charity," Locke insisted, "and without that faith which works, not by force, but by love." James Madison, a great student of Locke, warned that state-run religion "shackles and debilitates the mind" and "unfits it for every noble enterprise."

It seems that the freedom deficit in the Islamic world not only has inflamed the Muslim mind. It has rendered many minds devoid of charity, and made them unfit for the faith to recognize what is noble, decent and humane—the only kind of faith worth having.

13

Anti-Americanism Is a Trend

Claudio Veliz

Claudio Veliz is an author and history scholar.

Anti-Americanism is a trend rather than a radical movement. In fashionable culture capitals of the world, anti-Americanism is "in" and can be appropriately described as "anti-American chic." Although the rise of the United States is a powerful exhibition of democracy at work that has established countless academic, scientific, and artistic institutions, voguish contempt for the nation is leveled at a less edifying American export: popular culture. Beginning as a reaction spurred by military inferiority and U.S. support of Israel, anti-American chic is now perceived as a solemn duty to protect the world from the products of global industrial modernity.

The Manichean clarity of the Cold War has been sufficiently obscured by the rise of anti-Americanism to make it virtually impossible today to assume that all the then anti-communists are now staunch supporters of the United States, or to imagine that all those who regarded the Soviet Union as an inspiring portent of the future are now marching the streets of Paris, London, and Rome shouting obscenities against Mr. [George W.] Bush. Gone are the days when French, Swedish, Portuguese, or Italian anti-Americanism was a mandatory, blue-collar, political by-product of the Cold War. It is now a commonplace that suspicion, if not outright dislike, of the United States and everything it represents derive disconcerting

Claudio Veliz, "Industrial Modernity and its Anti-Americanisms," *National Observer—Australia and World Affairs*, vol. 69, Winter 2006, pp. 12–22. Copyright © 2006 Council for the National Interest. Reproduced by permission.

nourishment not only from the intelligentsia but from the higher reaches of some of the more prosperous and stable societies of the Western world. At the same time, the youth of the newly affluent working classes of these same countries— even when retaining faint memories of the compulsory anti-Americanism of the Cold War years—succumb happily to the embrace of the cultural creations of the colossus of the New World.

Unlike those Muslim countries where religion and politics coalesce and a robust and undifferentiated hatred of the great Satan is shared by all ranks, the anti-Americanism of the more advanced Western nations is characteristically diversified. It has spawned at least one influential variant that appears to be class-specific and has regaled the Western tradition with a breathtakingly original, latter-day extension of [author] Tom Wolfe's seminal concept of "radical chic."

In today's fashionable quarters of Paris, Berlin, and Brussels, anti-Americanist chic is "in."

The operative word here is not "radical", but "chic". Just as it was considered wildly audacious to sip Martinis with leather-clad Black Panthers in the Manhattan penthouses of the 1960s, or exchange pleasantries with Symbionese Liberation Army volunteers while wondering how the kids were getting along with their Weathermen buddies, in today's fashionable quarters of Paris, Berlin, and Brussels, anti-Americanist chic is "in," and not just with the useful idiots of the Cold War years. Considerable numbers of otherwise sane and respectable people are pouring obloquy on the United States, casting doubts on the intellectual acumen of President Bush, dismissing [former U.S. Secretary of State] Colin Powell as a kind of Uncle Tom and [current U.S. Secretary of State] Condoleezza Rice as an apprentice to [former British Primer Minister] Mrs. Thatcher and a traitor to gender and race.

Tom Wolfe observed that the great [conductor] Leonard ("Lenny") Bernstein and his friends favoured earthy, primitive, exotic, romantic, and preferably muscular radicalisms— qualities not readily associated with the American vanguard of industrial modernity, but dynamic Western society often takes astonishing turns, and this one certainly deserves to find its way into the history books under its proper name: "anti-American chic."

The swift rise of anti-American chic has brought about a surfeit of hand-wringing and teeth-gnashing explanations that, given the urgencies of the moment, have unfailingly attended to the contingent and the particular, such as the Kyoto episode, the retention of capital punishment, the International Criminal Court, American "unilateralism," the legal status of the Guantanamo inmates, and, of course, envy of the prosperity and power of the United States rather than to less publicised antecedents and long-term factors, some of which may deserve closer examination.

Notable social and economic achievement has not been at the expense of American excellence in the realm of "high culture."

The First Truly Prosperous Working Class

Such factors are mostly associated with the genesis and consequences, some quite unintended, of the English Industrial Revolution and the resulting cultural tidal-wave of industrial modernity, the swift progress of which is now popularly lampooned under the label of "globalisation." Less attention has been directed to the fact that the term refers to the virtual universalisation of cultural artifacts and social habits that, almost without exception, carry an imprimatur of aggressive vulgarity consistent with the tastes and preferences of the first affluent working class in world history. It must be added that this notable social and economic achievement has not been at the expense of American excellence in the realm of "high culture." This is confirmed by the many magnificent concert halls and opera companies; splendid museums and universities; and scientific and technological institutions that adorn a continuing industrial revolution tempered in its execution and results by remarkably successful sui generis democratic arrangements. These arrangements were bruised somewhat by a sanguinary civil war and are modified from time to time in response to contemporary usage and exigencies, but have certainly stood the test of time far better than those of every major nation outside the English-speaking world.

The problem is that good laws efficiently and fairly administered, successful voluntary organisations, clubs and neighborhood or national associations of patchwork-quilters, skiers, anarchists, vintage car collectors, socialists, orchid-growers, bungee jumpers, ornithologists, mountain climbers, cake-decorators, and Esperanto speakers, as well as the immensely civilised civic and political ambit that enables all these diverse activities to prosper, are not readily exportable and certainly lack the visibility and undemanding acceptability of, say, blue jeans, rap, skateboards, baseball caps, exposed navels, poker, tattoos, soft drinks, hamburgers, Broadway musicals, jazz, chewing gum, breast implants, skyscrapers, basketball, hot dogs, and the Internet.

What our world has witnessed during the past half century is a process of elective affinities of global proportions that has irreversibly modified the cultural landscape. The manner of this transformation has by now become almost predictable, with the sons and daughters of the working classes of the more prosperous Western nations steadily and effortlessly moving away from hallowed traditional loyalties and habits of consumption and embracing instead the emphatically vulgar cultural artifacts and dispositions of their generational counterparts in Chicago, Liverpool, Los Angeles and Cincinnati. The aggressiveness of this massive process of acculturation cannot be overlooked; but it is an aggressiveness consistent with the aplomb and creativity of the first truly prosperous working class, a free people as full of self-confidence as they are lacking in self-consciousness.

During the Cold War, the mostly inelegant excesses of Hollywood, Las Vegas, San Francisco and Madison Avenue; the American military presence (over-paid, over-sexed and over here); and the increasingly visible and very audible flood of American tourists, were condescendingly tolerated by the upper social strata of Brussels, Paris, Frankfurt and Florence. Their displeasure was muffled by the keen awareness that putting up with these unfortunate imports—clear evidence of American industrial, cultural and military vitality—was a reasonable price to pay for the security they enjoyed sheltered behind the only credible bulwark against international communism. With the end of the Cold War, the high tide of fear-induced harmony and good-fellowship has gradually receded, exposing ragged peaks of cultural contempt.

On its own, this cultural contempt would probably have been ignored, either because of habit or good manners, but it has been transformed into vociferous anti-American chic because of a number of other contemporary developments, of which the most important is probably the emergence of an "Old Europe" leadership intent on transforming the European Union into a countervailing power that will bring the upstart Americans to heel. This influence of an EU led by France and Germany has attracted deserved attention and does not need reiteration. However, there are three additional factors that do justify consideration: the contrast between the appalling military record of the dominant European nations and the military might sustained by the most powerful economy in world history; the latent anti-Semitism of the upper reaches of European society; and the realisation by the invariably left-leaning members of the intelligentsia that now they can, with impunity, place the blame for the eclipse of the joys of traditional *Gemeinschaft* community and the abuse of natural resources on the shoulders of the English-speaking vanguard of industrialism.

Military Aspects

The first additional factor to be considered concerns military aspects of the current world order. The banal observation that great economic power can translate into formidable military clout does not tell the whole story. If this were the whole story, its importance would be both obvious and limited. The paradoxical military histories of the dominant Western European nations suggest that wounded pride can fester into unrelieved acrimony that makes an impression among the ruling groups of the political spectrum.

It is astonishing that the two great nations of the West with the nicest military uniforms, the shiniest boots, the best martial music and parades, the most elegant headgear, and the most moving chronicles of battles fought are also encumbered with the least impressive record in military matters. When did Germany last win a war? In 1870, Germany defeated France when, after Sedan, large numbers of mules, horses, guns, soldiers, officers, generals, and one emperor fell into the hands of Bismarck and Kaiser Wilhelm I. This momentous victory invited a repetition that has proved as costly as it has been elusive. As for France, unless the inglorious impasse at the Crimea or the pathetic retreat from Mexico (where much of the fighting was left to the Foreign Legion) are declared victories, Wagram, in 1809, appears to be the last battle clearly won by the French (albeit under Corsican leadership). As for their last victory in a fully-fledged war waged without assistance from loyal and powerful allies, we must go back to the high school version of the 1679 Peace of Nijmegen, with Louis XIV emerging on top, though the French victory in the Dutch Wars is questionable. This means that the Germans have been denied military victories for 136 years, while the hapless French have endured 327 years of defeats. The usual apologies apply, of course, but the phrase "punch-drunk" comes to mind to describe societies so painfully bereft of the one kind of glory that they appear sincerely to value.

To be trounced at war is not a trivial matter, and regardless of how courageously a nation endures the unendurable, a succession of defeats, in addition to widows and orphans, must have emotional consequences (ranging from feelings of inadequacy to outright resentment) that probably offend the collective conscience in ways as difficult to gauge as they are to overcome. Such feelings are unlikely to vanish when crumbling French armies are rescued by large numbers of English-speaking soldiers, not once, but twice in a few decades. Even less so when the economic chaos left by the most recent and massive defeat, in the Second World War, is also put right by generous handouts from the same English-speaking source. Finally, if this insulting generosity, piled on top of the original battlefield humiliation, was not enough, the subsequent disinclination or inability, or both, of these countries to provide for their own defence has made it necessary, and largely at their own request, for many thousands of English-speaking soldiers to remain in Europe for more than half a century. For nations so eager to glorify a sobering military past, circumstances such as these can be trying, especially among those upper-class circles whose appreciation of military prowess seems to be more earnest than, say that normally found among coat-miners, peasants and stevedores.

There is little doubt that anti-Semitism, latent or otherwise, has found in anti-American chic a most convenient ally for the trek back into social respectability.

Anti-Semitism and Industrial Modernity

The second additional factor to be considered is anti-Semitism. There is little doubt that anti-Semitism, latent or otherwise, has found in anti-American chic a most convenient ally for the trek back into social respectability. This is at least in part because it is possible to interpret the crisis in the Middle East as one pitting the United States and Israel against countries and forces associated directly or indirectly with terrorist activities. There is no need to invoke the Dreyfus episode, the policies of the Vichy regime, the Cremieux Crisis or the contemporary German attempts to address their own "Jewish question", to conjecture that the anti-Semitism now reappearing in the upper reaches of French and German societies was dormant there all the time. It is not difficult to understand why, during the Cold War, it was considered offensive, impolite or inopportune to air such views, since the business at hand was to keep the Soviet threat within bounds with the help of decisively anti-communist and well-armed countries such as the United States and Israel. At present, however, the revived anti-Semitism is acquiring an odd kind of acceptance by hanging on to the coat-tails of anti-American chic. This is especially true of the upper layers of French and German society where forceful reservations about Israel's policies, approval of the Palestinian position, and doubts about the unhappy consequences—they include September 11 among these—of American support for Israel have become the flavour of the season.

The third factor that invites consideration is the transition from *Gemeinschaft* (or communal) to *Gesellschaft* (or associational) social arrangements, arguably the most challenging and irreversible consequence of the advance of industrial modernity. This was first observed and given system and nomenclature by the founding fathers of the modern study of society. From Comte, Marx and Durkheim, to Weber, Le Play and Tonnies, these thinkers helped to establish the idea of community, and especially of community lost as an indispensable component of any attempt to understand the complexities of the social impact of the English Industrial Revolution. The argument is both simple and compelling. At the heart of the continuing Industrial Revolution, and the resulting culture of industrial modernity, is a process of change driven forward relentlessly by the technological applications and concomitant economic and social adjustments of an expanding frontier of scientific knowledge. This need not be a prescription for historical determinism, but can be simply a complex, interactive, and obviously indeterminate fact with each of these changes demanding recombinations of land, capital and labour—the three classical factors of production—and thereby impressing on each a necessary and unprecedented social and spatial mobility. This brings about a generalised substitution of rational, elective, and mostly ephemeral *Gesellschaft*, or associational arrangements, for the traditionally tightly structured, pre-industrial *Gemeinschaft* community.

This is Sociology 101 stuff that, interpreted by [dictators] Lenin, Stalin, Mao and Pol Pot, brought death to many millions of human beings and became an integral item of the ideological baggage of the left-wing intelligentsia until the collapse of the Soviet Union. Marx saw with lethal clarity that traditional *Gemeinschaft* community stood everywhere and in every conceivable way as an obstacle to what he believed to be the inevitable progress towards a communist society of equals. Decisively distancing himself from [writer] Oliver Goldsmith's idyllic vision in his poem "The Deserted Village", he wrenched traditional community away from the cloying sentimentality of the romantics and defined it anew as the exemplary symbol of the oppressive darkness of irrational loyalties and affections, tradition, and superstition. Writing about social change in India, he explained that "we must not forget that these idyllic village communities . . . restrained the human mind within the smallest possible compass, making it the unrelenting tool of superstition, enslaving it beneath traditional rules." And applauding the bourgeois revolution that transformed European society since the sixteenth century, he stated that "it set free the political spirit which had, so to speak, been dissolved, fragmented, and lost in the various cul de sacs of feudal society." These blind alleys that impeded the march of history included the family, all forms of local and regional allegiance, vocational or hereditary loyalty to occupation, guild affiliations, and, of course, the claims of religion. Such a robust rejection of every kind of customary human arrangement supplied the firm theoretical foundation for his approval of the "giant broom" of a French Revolution that had swept all the communal rubbish into the proverbial dustbin of history.

A Hallowed Duty

Throughout the sombre years of the Cold War, this principal theoretical instruction was followed to the letter. The onerous task of conserving traditional values and institutions was left exclusively to conservatives, who found few allies among the ranks of revolutionary workers, peasants and soldiers—let alone among an intelligentsia that was loudly advancing the creation of day-care centres as a substitute for the outmoded comforts and affections of family life, and the international solidarity of the proletariat as an adequate antidote for the rising tide of twentieth-century regionalisms and nationalisms.

Things have changed mightily since the crumbling of the Soviet Union and the discrediting of its theoretical and conceptual scaffolding. These momentous events have in turn resulted in some astonishing reconsiderations and realignments under new battle flags. But none are as bizarre as the one that has led to the intimate cohabitation of the European left-wing intelligentsia with the traditionalist, conservative, anti-American chic devotees of Western Europe. The cement that now binds together such seemingly incompatible partners is their visceral hatred of the United States—in one, the shop-soiled remnant of the best years of the Cold War; in the other, the fiery passion rightly reserved for those emerging from closets or perceiving the light en route to Damascus. Only a few years ago, Marxist intellectuals were lustily defending Mao's cultural revolution, justifying the pitiless obliteration of village traditions, the re-education of Cambodian deviationists, and the robust rejection of reactionary sentimental flotsam, such as conjugal love, friendship, and national loyalty. The very same intellectuals are now rediscovering the therapeutic charms of unhurried village life; the creative pleasures of arts and crafts; the joys of tree-hugging holidays and country cooking; and the satisfaction of counting [former French president] M. Chirac as their very own comrade in arms. As can be imagined, their upper-class bedfellows are as impressed by the heart-warming devotion of the intellectual leaders of the proletariat to decaying manor houses, herbaceous borders, ancient music, and private schools as they are by the unhesitant and generous way in which their new friends have understood, indeed applauded, their own reservations about Israel and the mysterious activities of the Zionists, their steadfast defence of national honour and the purity of the language against American inroads, their qualified admiration for [Cuban dictator] Fidel Castro and [Libyan leader] Colonel Gaddafi, and their staunch rejection of Colonel Sanders fried chicken, the Internet, McDonald's hamburgers, Disney theme parks, Hollywood films, baseball caps worn backwards, and the invasion of Iraq.

Anti-American chic [is] vastly more than an aesthetic rejection of dry sandwiches and bad music.

However, the true shock of revelation came when in due course their shared enjoyment of anti-American chic gave birth to the realisation that the heartless homogenisation of everything; the sartorial imperialism; the unregulated distribution of immoral, violent and wildly popular films; the irresponsible scientific advances and technological applications; the continuing recombinations of the forces of production; the plague of consumerism shamelessly encouraged by indiscriminate affluence, social mobility, and air-conditioned shopping malls; the obliteration of *Gemeinschaft* community; and, most importantly, a corrupting globalisation that threatens fatally to divert the March of History, are all creatures of the English-speaking vanguard of industrial modernity—especially of the United States. It became clear across the Western European political spectrum that anti-American chic was vastly more than an aesthetic rejection of dry sandwiches and bad music. It has now been embraced as a hallowed duty— the only morally progressive response to the anguished appeals of [Greek muse of history] Clio herself, abused, aggrieved, and badly let down by Russian ineptitude, to help defend her European homeland against the advancing gender-neutral, jogging, blue-jeaned, foul-mouthed, T-shirted, and hip hopping vulgarian hordes.

Organizations to Contact

The editors have compiled the following list of organizations concerned with the issues debated in this book. The descriptions are derived from materials provided by the organizations. All have publications or information available for interested readers. The list was compiled on the date of publication of the present volume; names, addresses, phone and fax numbers, and e-mail addresses may change. Be aware that many organizations take several weeks or longer to respond to inquiries, so allow as much time as possible.

American Enterprise Institute
1150 17th St. NW, Washington, DC   20036
(202) 862-5800 • fax: (202) 862-7177
Web site: www.aei.org

The American Enterprise Institute for Public Policy Research is a scholarly research institute that is dedicated to preserving a strong foreign policy and national defense. Articles, speeches, and seminar transcripts on American foreign relations are available on its Web site.

Brookings Institution
1775 Massachusetts Ave. NW, Washington, DC   20036
(202) 797-6000
Web site: www.brookings.org

The Brookings Institution is a think tank that conducts research and education in foreign policy, economics, government, and the social sciences. Its Saban Center for Middle East Policy develops programs to promote a better understanding of policy choices in the Middle East. Articles on American foreign relations can be found on the organization's Web site and in its publications, including the quarterly *Brookings Review*.

Cato Institute

1000 Massachusetts Ave. NW, Washington, DC   20001-5403
(202) 842-0200 • fax: (202) 842-3490
Web site: www.cato.org

The Cato Institute is a libertarian public-policy research foundation dedicated to limiting the role of government and promoting free markets and peace. It disapproves of an interventionist foreign policy and believes that the use of U.S. forces in other countries should be limited. The institute publishes the quarterly magazine *Regulation*, the bimonthly *Cato Policy Report*, and numerous papers dealing with foreign policy.

Center for Strategic and International Studies

1800 K St. NW, Washington, DC   20006
(202) 887-0200 • fax: (202) 775-3199
Web site: www.csis.org

The center works to provide world leaders with strategic insights and policy options on current and emerging global issues. It publishes books, international affairs journal *The Washington Quarterly*, and other publications, including reports that can be downloaded from its Web site.

Council on Foreign Relations

58 E. 68th St., New York, NY   10065
(212) 434-9400 • fax: (212) 434-9800
e-mail: communications@cfr.org
Web site: www.cfr.org

The council specializes in foreign affairs and studies the international aspects of American political and economic policies and problems. Its journal *Foreign Affairs*, published five times a year, includes analyses of America's relations with countries around the world.

Foreign Policy Association

470 Park Ave. South, New York, NY   10016
(212) 481-8100 • fax: (212) 481-9275

e-mail: info@fpa.org

Web site: www.fpa.org

The Foreign Policy Association is a nonprofit organization that believes a concerned and informed public is the foundation for an effective foreign policy. Publications such as the annual *Great Decisions* briefing book and the quarterly *Headline Series* review U.S. foreign policy issues in China, the Persian Gulf and the Middle East, and Africa.

Heritage Foundation

214 Massachusetts Ave. NE, Washington, DC 20002-4999

(202) 546-4400 • fax: (202) 546-8328

e-mail: info@heritage.org

Web site: www.heritage.org

The Heritage Foundation is a conservative public-policy research institute. Its position papers and reports on America's foreign policy include "Why America Is Such a Hard Sell: Beyond Pride and Prejudice" and "Bush's Global Cultural Initiative: A Step Toward Revitalizing U.S. Public Diplomacy."

Hoover Institution

434 Galvez Mall, Stanford, CA 94305-6010

(650) 723-1754 • fax: (650) 723-1687

Web site: www.hoover.org

The Hoover Institution is a public-policy research center devoted to advanced study of politics, economics, and international affairs. It publishes the quarterly *Hoover Digest* and *Policy Review*—which often includes articles on American foreign relations—as well as a newsletter and special reports, including "Foreign Policy for America in the Twenty-first Century."

Institute for Policy Studies

1112 16th St., Suite 600, Washington, DC 20036

(202) 234-9382

e-mail: info@ips-dc.org
Web site: www.ips-dc.org

The Institute for Policy Studies is a progressive think tank that works to develop societies built around the values of justice and nonviolence. It publishes reports, including "The Iraq War: The Cost to States" and "Military vs. Climate Security."

Iraq Action Coalition
7309 Haymarket Ln., Raleigh, NC   27615
fax: (919) 846-7422
e-mail: iac@leb.net
Web site: www.iraqaction.org

The Iraq Action Coalition is an online resource center for groups and activists who opposed both international economic sanctions and U.S. military action against Iraq. It publishes books and reports on Iraq, including *Iraq Under Siege: The Deadly Impact of Sanctions and War*. Its Web site includes numerous links to other organizations opposed to the war against Iraq.

Middle East Forum
1500 Walnut St., Suite 1050, Philadelphia, PA   19102
(215) 546-5406
Web site: www.meforum.org

The Middle East Forum is a think tank that works to define and promote American interests in the Middle East. It supports strong American ties with Israel, Turkey, and other democracies as they emerge. It publishes *Middle East Quarterly*, a policy-oriented journal. Its Web site includes articles, summaries of activities, and a discussion forum.

Middle East Institute
1761 N St. NW, Washington, DC   20036-2882
(202) 785-1141 • fax: (202) 331-8861
e-mail: mideasti@mideasti.org
Web site: www.themiddleeastinstitute.org

The institute's charter mission is to promote better understanding of Middle Eastern cultures, languages, religions, and politics. It publishes numerous books, papers, audiotapes, and videos as well as the quarterly *Middle East Journal*. It also maintains an educational outreach department to give teachers and students of all grade levels advice on resources.

Trilateral Commission
1156 15th St. NW, Washington, DC   20005
(202) 467-5410 • fax: (202) 467-5415
e-mail: contactus@trilateral.org
Web site: www.trilateral.org

The commission encourages shared leadership responsibilities among the countries in North America, Western Europe, and Japan. It publishes the annual magazine *Trialogue*.

United Nations
UN Headquarters, New York, NY   10017
Web site: www.un.org

The United Nations (UN) is an international organization dedicated to maintaining international peace and security, developing friendly relations among nations, and promoting international cooperation. Articles and speeches about American foreign relations are available on its Web site.

Bibliography

Books

Richard Z. Chesnof	*The Arrogance of the French: Why They Can't Stand Us—And Why the Feeling Is Mutual.* New York: Sentinel Trade, 2006.
Robert Corfe	*Freedom from America: For Safeguarding Democracy and the Economic and Cultural Integrity of Peoples.* Bury St. Edmunds, UK: Arena Books, 2006.
Richard Crockatt	*After 9/11: Cultural Dimensions of American Global Power.* New York: Routledge, 2007.
Sigrid Faath, ed.	*Anti-Americanism in the Islamic World.* Princeton, NJ: Markus Wiener, 2006.
Richard Higgott and Ivona Malbasic, eds.	*The Political Consequences of Anti-Americanism.* New York: Routledge, 2008.
Johny K. Johansson	*In Your Face: How American Marketing Excess Fuels Anti-Americanism.* Upper Saddle River, NJ: Prentice Hall, 2004.
Andrew Kohut and Bruce Stokes	*America Against the World: How We Are Different and Why We Are Disliked.* New York: Times Books, 2006.

110

| Kishore Mahbubani | *Beyond the Age of Innocence: A Worldly View of America.* New York: Public Affairs, 2005. |

| Andrei S. Markovits | *Uncouth Nation: Why Europe Dislikes America.* Princeton, NJ: Princeton University Press, 2007. |

| John Harmon McElroy | *Divided We Stand: The Rejection of American Culture Since the 1960s.* Lanham, MD: Rowman & Littlefield, 2006. |

| Nancy Snow | *The Arrogance of American Power: What U.S. Leaders Are Doing Wrong and Why It's Our Duty to Dissent.* Lanham, MD: Rowman & Littlefield, 2006. |

Periodicals

| James W. Ceasar | "Anti-Americanism, Ever with Us: Reflecting on a Stubborn Ideology," *National Review*, April 30, 2007. |

| *The Economist* | "Still Not Loved. Now Not Envied; How Others See Americans. (Who Loves Ya, Baby?)," *Economist*, June 25, 2005. |

| Mark Falcoff | "Remember the Maine; Not Much Love Lost Between the United States and Spain," *Weekly Standard*, February 11, 2008. |

| Michael Gerson | "A Popularity Offensive," *Washington Post*, March 7, 2008. |

Neil Gross   "The Many Stripes of Anti-Americanism," *Boston Globe*, January 14, 2007.

Peter Gumber   "Branding America: Why on Earth Are U.S. Companies Handing Out Diplomacy Guides?" *Time*, February 28, 2005.

Gary Kamiya   "Of War and Cancer," Salon.com, March 17, 2008.

Fred Kaplan   "Downsizing Our Dominance," *Los Angeles Times*, February 2, 2008.

J.F.O. McAllister   "Drifting Apart," *Time*, October 1, 2006.

Manuel Parapan   "Why Arabs Are Anti-U.S." *World & I*, January 2005.

John Pilger   "Who Hates Michael Moore?" *New Statesmen*, October 22, 2007.

Clay Risen   "Remaindered: The Decline of Brand America," *New Republic*, April 11, 2005.

Michael Slackman   "Warmth for Americans in Once Hostile Iran," *New York Times*, February 13, 2008.

Irwin Stelzer   "America: You'll Miss It When It's Gone," *Spectator*, March 3, 2007.

Hubert Vedrine   "On Anti-Americanism," *Brown Journal of World Affairs*, Winter–Spring 2004.

James Zogby   "Mutual Misconception: Arabs Need
a Lot More Public Diplomacy in the
U.S." *International Herald Tribune*,
July 5, 2006.

Index

anti-American ideology, 36–38, 73
Bush administration and, 71, 72
European Union, 37, 97
"Europeanism," 82–83
holidays of Americanized, 81
identity politics of, 37–38, 82
as pro-American, 86–88
United Nations and, 38–39

F

Faber, Klaus, 76
Fahrenheit 911 (film), 48
FBI, 47
Fernandez, Alberto, 33, 34
First Gulf War, 28
Foreign Policy Association, 106–107
France
  anti-Americanism of, 37
  military record, 98–99
  U.S. medium-range missiles and, 72
Franco, Francisco, 36
French Revolution, 102
Friedman, Thomas, 31–32
Friendly Fire (Sweig), 28
Full Metal Jacket (film), 47

G

Gabler, Neil, 45
Garfield: A Tale of Two Kitties (film), 51
Gemeinschaft, 100, 101, 104
German Marshal Fund, 58, 85, 86, 87
Germany
  American legal system and, 81
  education and, 79–81
  military record, 98

moral relativism of, 36–37
terrorist plot and, 89
Gesellschaft, 100, 101
Global Islamic Media Front, 30
Global Research in International Affairs, 8
Globalization, 10, 21, 95
Goldsmith, Oliver, 101
The Green Berets (film), 47
Guantanamo (detention center in Cuba), 26, 73
The Guardian (newspaper), 77, 80
Gulag (Soviet Union), 47
Gulf War. *See* First Gulf War

H

Haller, Gret, 75
Halloween, 81
Hamburg, Germany, 81
Harry Potter, 51
Hating America: A History (Rubin), 26
He Wears a Pair of Silver Wings (song), 46
Healthcare, 66
Heritage Foundation, 107
Hi (magazine)
Hillsborough Stadium, Sheffield, England, 77
Hiroshima, Japan, 59, 65
A History of the English-Speaking Peoples Since 1900 (Roberts), 48
Hollywood
  creating anti-Americanism, 45–49
  engine of American economy, 51
  not creating anti-Americanism, 50–52
  popularity of products, 51, 52
  as storyteller, 42–43

DATE